ROLAND BARTHES was born in 1915. He is now a Professor at the Collège de France, Paris. Among his books are *Le degré zéro de l'écriture* (*Writing Degree Zero*), 1953; *Mythologies* (*Mythologies*), 1957; *Eléments de sémiologie* (*Elements of Semiology*), 1964; *S/Z* (*S/Z*), 1970; *L'Empire des signes*, 1970; *Sade, Fourier, Loyola* (*Sade, Fourier, Loyola*), 1971; *Barthes par lui-même*, 1975; *Fragments d'un discours amoureux*, 1977.

STEPHEN HEATH was educated at Jesus College, Cambridge, and the Ecole Pratique des Hautes Etudes, Paris. He has been a Fellow of Jesus College and a University Lecturer at Cambridge since 1969. He has also been a member of the *Corps Enseignant Littéraire* at the Ecole Normale Supérieure in Paris since 1975. He is the author of *The Nouveau Roman: a study in the practice of writing* (1972) and *Vertige du déplacement* (1974).

Fontana Communications Series

EDITED BY RAYMOND WILLIAMS

IMAGE

MUSIC

TEXT

ROLAND BARTHES

Essays selected and translated by
Stephen Heath

Fontana Paperbacks

First published in Fontana 1977
Third impression January 1982

Copyright © Roland Barthes 1977
English Translation © Stephen Heath 1977

Made and printed in Great Britain by
William Collins Sons & Co. Ltd, Glasgow

Illustrations I, XI, XII, XIII, XIV and XV are
from the collection of Vincent Pinel.

Contents

Translator's Note

Leaving aside the problems involved in any translation, special difficulties arise when (as here) there is (as yet?) no real overlap in theoretical context between the two languages in question. With regard to the semiological reference in these essays, I have tried wherever possible to conform to the terminological solutions adopted by the English translators of Barthes's *Elements of Semiology*. A certain amount of bibliographical – and occasionally explanatory – material has been added in footnotes which are identified by being placed in square brackets.

The following terms pose particular difficulties:

Langue/parole – The reference here is to the distinction made by the Swiss linguist Saussure. Where *parole* is the realm of the individual moments of language use, of particular 'utterances' or 'messages', whether spoken or written, *langue* is the system or code ('*le code de la langue*') which allows the realization of the individual messages. As the language-system, object of linguistics, *langue* is thus also to be differentiated from *langage*, the heterogeneous totality with which the linguist is initially faced and which may be studied from a variety of points of view, partaking as it does of the physical, the physiological, the mental, the individual and the social. It is precisely by delimiting its specific object and fixing as its task the description of that object (that is, of the *langue*, the system of the language) that Saussure founds linguistics as a science. (Chomsky's distinction between *competence/performance* – 'the speaker-hearer's knowledge of his language' and 'the actual use of language in concrete situations' – resembles that between *langue/parole* but, so to speak, brings within the scope of *langue* elements – the recursive processes underlying sentence formation – regarded by Saussure as belonging to *parole*). The problem in translation is that in English 'language' has to serve for both *langue* and *langage*. *Langue* can often be specified by translation as 'a' or 'the language' or again as 'language-system' (in opposition to the 'language-use' of parole), but I have included the French term in brackets in cases where the idea of the analytic construction of a language-system is being given crucial stress (see notably the 'Introduction to the structural analysis of narratives').

Enoncé/énonciation – Both these terms are often translated in English as 'utterance', but whereas the first signifies what is uttered (the statement, the proposition), the second signifies the act of uttering (the act of speech, writing or whatever by which the statement is stated, the proposition proposed). This distinction rejoins *and displaces* that between *langue/parole*: every *énoncé* is a piece of *parole*; consideration of *énonciation* involves not only the social and psychological (i.e. non-linguistic) context of *énoncés*, but also features of *langue* itself, of the ways in which it structures the possibilities of *énonciation* (symbol-indexes such as personal pronouns, tenses, anaphores are the most obvious of these linguistic features of *énonciation*). The distinction – the displacement – has particular importance in any – semiological, psychoanalytical, textual – attention to the passage, the divisions, of the subject in language, in the symbolic, to the slide seized in the disjunction of the *sujet de l'énoncé* and the *sujet de l'énonciation*. In the utterance 'I am lying', for example, it is evident that the subject of the proposition is not one with the subject of the enunciation of the proposition – the 'I' cannot lie on both planes at once. Dream, lapsus and joke are so many disorders of the regulation of these planes, of the exchange between subject and signifier; as too, exactly, is the *text*. The distinction *énoncé/énonciation* is rendered here, according to context, either by 'statement' or 'proposition'/ 'utterance' or, more simply and carefully, by 'enounced'/ 'enunciation'.

Plaisir/jouissance – English lacks a word able to carry the range of meaning in the term *jouissance* which includes enjoyment in the sense of a legal or social possession (enjoy certain rights, enjoy a privilege), pleasure, and, crucially, the pleasure of sexual climax. The problem would be less acute were it not that *jouissance* is specifically contrasted to *plaisir* by Barthes in his *Le Plaisir du texte*: on the one hand a pleasure (*plaisir*) linked to cultural enjoyment and identity, to the cultural enjoyment of identity, to a homogenizing movement of the ego; on the other a radically violent pleasure (*jouissance*) which shatters – dissipates, loses – that cultural identity, that ego. The American translation of *Le Plaisir du texte* (*The Pleasure of the Text*, New York 1975) uses the word 'bliss' for *jouissance*; the success of this is dubious, however, since not only does 'bliss' lack an effective verbal form (to render the French *jouir*), it also brings with it connotations of religious and social contentment ('heavenly bliss', 'blissfully happy') which damagingly weaken the force of the original French term. I have no real answer to the problem and have resorted to a series of words which in different contexts can contain at least some of that force: 'thrill' (easily verbalized with 'to thrill', more physical and potentially sexual, than 'bliss'), 'climactic pleasure', 'come' and 'coming' (the exact sexual translation of *jouir*, *jouissance*), 'dissipation' (somewhat too moral in its judgement but able to render the *loss*, the fragmentation, emphasized by Barthes in *jouissance*).

Signifiance – A theoretical concept initially proposed and developed by Julia Kristeva (see *Semeiotiké: Recherches pour une sémanalyse*, Paris 1969; a brief account can be found in English in her 'The semiotic activity', *Screen* Vol. 14 No. 1/2, Spring/Summer 1973). *Signifiance* has sometimes been translated as 'significance', but this, with its assent to the stressed position of the sign, is exactly what it is not and it has here been left as *signifiance*. Barthes himself introduces *signifiance* as follows in a passage which gathers together a number of the terms that have been discussed in this present note: '. . . when the text is read (or written) as a moving play of signifiers, without any possible reference to one or some fixed signifieds, it becomes necessary to distinguish signification, which belongs to the plane of the product, of the enounced, of communication, and the work of the signifier, which belongs to the plane of the production, of the enunciation, of symbolization – this work being called *signifiance*. *Signifiance* is a *process* in the course of which the "subject" of the text, escaping the logic of the *ego-cogito* and engaging in other logics (of the signifier, of contradiction), struggles with meaning and is deconstructed ("lost"); *signifiance* – and this is what immediately distinguishes it from signification is thus precisely a *work*: not the work by which the (intact and exterior) subject might try to master the language (as, for example, by a work of style), but that radical work (leaving nothing intact) through which the subject explores – entering, not observing – how the language works and undoes him or her. *Signifiance* is "the un-end of possible operations in a given field of a language". Contrary to signification, *signifiance* cannot be reduced, therefore, to communication, representation, expression: it places the subject (of writer, reader) in the text not as a projection . . . but as a "loss", a "disappearance". Hence its identification with the pleasure of *jouissance*: the text becomes erotic through *signifiance* (no need, that is, for the text to represent erotic "scenes").'

Finally, it must be said that the relatively minor part played by grammatical gender in English, where the reference of the pronouns *he, she* and *it* is very largely determined by so-called 'natural' gender, creates difficulties when translating from an effectively grammatical gender language such as French: either one produces a text in which the masculine reference predominates or one specifies the feminine equally at every point (*he/she, him-or-herself*, etc.). The effect of the latter strategy – the signified determination to move against linguistic sexism – could only be an addition by the translator to Barthes's writing in French; for this reason alone, it has not been adopted here.

S.H.

Sources

Original titles and sources of the essays published in this collection are as follows:

The Photographic Message: 'Le message photographique', *Communications* 1, 1961.

Rhetoric of the Image: 'Rhétorique de l'image', *Communications* 4, 1964.

The Third Meaning: 'Le troisième sens: Notes de recherche sur quelques photogrammes de S. M. Eisenstein', *Cahiers du cinéma*, 222, 1970.

Diderot, Brecht, Eisenstein: 'Diderot, Brecht, Eisenstein', in *Cinéma, Théorie, Lectures* (special number of the *Revue d'esthétique*), 1973.

Introduction to the Structural Analysis of Narratives: 'Introduction à l'analyse structurale des récits', *Communications* 8, 1966.

The Struggle with the Angel: 'La lutte avec l'ange: Analyse textuelle de Genèse 32, 22–32', in *Analyse structurale et exégèse biblique*, Neuchâtel 1971.

The Death of the Author: 'La mort de l'auteur', *Mantéia* V, 1968.

Musica Practica: 'Musica practica', *L'Arc* 40, 1970.

From Work to Text: 'De l'œuvre au texte', *Revue d'esthétique* 3, 1971.

Change the Object Itself: 'Changer l'objet lui-même' (Barthes's title: 'La mythologie aujourd'hui'), *Esprit*, April 1971.

Lesson in Writing: 'Leçon d'écriture', *Tel Quel* 34, Summer 1968.

The Grain of the Voice: 'Le grain de la voix', *Musique en jeu* 9, 1972.

Writers, Intellectuals, Teachers: 'Ecrivains, intellectuels, professeurs', *Tel Quel* 47, Autumn 1971.

The Photographic Message

The press photograph is a message. Considered overall this message is formed by a source of emission, a channel of transmission and a point of reception. The source of emission is the staff of the newspaper, the group of technicians certain of whom take the photo, some of whom choose, compose and treat it, while others, finally, give it a title, a caption and a commentary. The point of reception is the public which reads the paper. As for the channel of transmission, this is the newspaper itself, or, more precisely, a complex of concurrent messages with the photograph as centre and surrounds constituted by the text, the title, the caption, the lay-out and, in a more abstract but no less 'informative' way, by the very name of the paper (this name represents a knowledge that can heavily orientate the reading of the message strictly speaking: a photograph can change its meaning as it passes from the very conservative *L'Aurore* to the communist *L'Humanité*). These observations are not without their importance for it can readily be seen that in the case of the press photograph the three traditional parts of the message do not call for the same method of investigation. The emission and the reception of the message both lie within the field of a sociology: it is a matter of studying human groups, of defining motives and attitudes, and of trying to link the behaviour of these groups to the social totality of which they are a part. For the message itself, however, the method is inevitably different: whatever the origin and the destination of the message, the photograph is not simply a product or a channel but also an object endowed with a structural autonomy. Without in any way intending to divorce this object from its use, it is necessary to provide for a specific method prior to sociological analysis and which can only be the immanent analysis of the unique structure that a photograph constitutes.

Naturally, even from the perspective of a purely immanent analysis, the structure of the photograph is not an isolated structure; it is in communication with at least one other structure, namely the text – title, caption or article – accompanying every press photograph. The totality of the information is thus carried by two different structures (one of which is linguistic). These two structures are co-operative but, since their units are heterogeneous, necessarily remain separate from one another: here (in the text) the substance of the message is made up of words; there (in the photograph) of lines, surfaces, shades. Moreover, the two structures of the message each occupy their own defined spaces, these being contiguous but not 'homogenized', as they are for example in the rebus which fuses words and images in a single line of reading. Hence, although a press photograph is never without a written commentary, the analysis must first of all bear on each separate structure; it is only when the study of each structure has been exhausted that it will be possible to understand the manner in which they complement one another. Of the two structures, one is already familiar, that of language (but not, it is true, that of the 'literature' formed by the language-use of the newspaper; an enormous amount of work is still to be done in this connection), while almost nothing is known about the other, that of the photograph. What follows will be limited to the definition of the initial difficulties in providing a structural analysis of the photographic message.

The photographic paradox

What is the content of the photographic message? What

does the photograph transmit? By definition, the scene itself, the literal reality. From the object to its image there is of course a reduction – in proportion, perspective, colour – but at no time is this reduction a *transformation* (in the mathematical sense of the term). In order to move from the reality to its photograph it is in no way necessary to divide up this reality into units and to constitute these units as signs, substantially different from the object they communicate; there is no necessity to set up a relay, that is to say a code, between the object and its image. Certainly the image is not the reality but at least it is its perfect *analogon* and it is exactly this analogical perfection which, to common sense, defines the photograph. Thus can be seen the special status of the photographic image: *it is a message without a code*; from which proposition an important corollary must immediately be drawn: the photographic message is a continuous message.

Are there other messages without a code? At first sight, yes: precisely the whole range of analogical reproductions of reality – drawings, paintings, cinema, theatre. In fact, however, each of those messages develops in an immediate and obvious way a supplementary message, in addition to the analogical content itself (scene, object, landscape), which is what is commonly called the *style* of the reproduction; second meaning, whose signifier is a certain 'treatment' of the image (result of the action of the creator) and whose signified, whether aesthetic or ideological, refers to a certain 'culture' of the society receiving the message. In short, all these 'imitative' arts comprise two messages: a *denoted* message, which is the *analogon* itself, and a *connoted* message, which is the manner in which the society to a certain extent communicates what it thinks of it. This duality of messages is evident in all reproductions other than photographic ones: there is no drawing, no matter how exact, whose very exactitude is not turned into a style (the style of 'verism'); no filmed scene whose objectivity is not finally read as the very sign of objectivity. Here again, the study of these connoted messages has still to be carried out (in particular it has to be decided whether what is called a work of art can be reduced to a system of significations); one can only anticipate that for all these imitative arts – when common – the code of the connoted system is very likely constituted either by a universal symbolic order or by a period rhetoric, in short by a stock of stereotypes (schemes, colours, graphisms, gestures, expressions, arrangements of elements).

When we come to the photograph, however, we find in principle nothing of the kind, at any rate as regards the press photograph (which is never an 'artistic' photograph). The photograph professing to be a mechanical analogue of reality, its first-order message in some sort completely fills its substance and leaves no place for the development of a second-order message. Of all the structures of information[1], the photograph appears as the only one that is exclusively constituted and occupied by a 'denoted' message, a message which totally exhausts its mode of existence. In front of a photograph, the feeling of 'denotation', or, if one prefers, of analogical plenitude, is so great that the description of a photograph is literally impossible; *to describe* consists precisely in joining to the denoted message a relay or second-order message derived from a code which is that of language and constituting in relation to the photographic analogue, however much care one takes to be exact, a connotation: to describe is thus not simply to be imprecise or incomplete, it is to change structures, to

1. It is a question, of course, of 'cultural' or culturalized structures, not of operational structures. Mathematics, for example, constitutes a denoted structure without any connotation at all; should mass society seize on it, however, setting out for instance an algebraic formula in an article on Einstein, this originally purely mathematical message now takes on a very heavy connotation, since it *signifies* science.

signify something different to what is shown.[1]

This purely 'denotative' status of the photograph, the perfection and plenitude of its analogy, in short its 'objectivity', has every chance of being mythical (these are the characteristics that common sense attributes to the photograph). In actual fact, there is a strong probability (and this will be a working hypothesis) that the photographic message too – at least in the press – is connoted. Connotation is not necessarily immediately graspable at the level of the message itself (it is, one could say, at once invisible and active, clear and implicit) but it can already be inferred from certain phenomena which occur at the levels of the production and reception of the message: on the one hand, the press photograph is an object that has been worked on, chosen, composed, constructed, treated according to professional, aesthetic or ideological norms which are so many factors of connotation; while on the other, this same photograph is not only perceived, received, it is *read*, connected more or less consciously by the public that consumes it to a traditional stock of signs. Since every sign supposes a code, it is this code (of connotation) that one should try to establish. The photographic paradox can then be seen as the co-existence of two messages, the one without a code (the photographic analogue), the other with a code (the 'art', or the treatment, or the 'writing', or the rhetoric, of the photograph); structurally, the paradox is clearly not the collusion of a denoted message and a connoted message (which is the – probably inevitable – status of all the forms of mass communication), it is that here the connoted (or coded) message develops on the basis of a message *without a code*. This structural paradox coincides with an ethical paradox: when one wants to be 'neutral', 'objective', one

1. The description of a drawing is easier, involving, finally, the description of a structure that is already connoted, fashioned with a *coded* signification in view. It is for this reason perhaps that psychological texts use a great many drawings and very few photographs.

strives to copy reality meticulously, as though the analogical were a factor of resistance against the investment of values (such at least is the definition of aesthetic 'realism'); how then can the photograph be at once 'objective' and 'invested', natural and cultural? It is through an understanding of the mode of imbrication of denoted and connoted messages that it may one day be possible to reply to that question. In order to undertake this work, however, it must be remembered that since the denoted message in the photograph is absolutely analogical, which is to say *continuous*, outside of any recourse to a code, there is no need to look for the signifying units of the first-order message; the connoted message on the contrary does comprise a plane of expression and a plane of content, thus necessitating a veritable decipherment. Such a decipherment would as yet be premature, for in order to isolate the signifying units and the signified themes (or values) one would have to carry out (perhaps using tests) directed readings, artificially varying certain elements of a photograph to see if the variations of forms led to variations in meaning. What can at least be done now is to forecast the main planes of analysis of photographic connotation.

Connotation procedures

Connotation, the imposition of second meaning on the photographic message proper, is realized at the different levels of the production of the photograph (choice, technical treatment, framing, lay-out) and represents, finally, a coding of the photographic analogue. It is thus possible to separate out various connotation procedures, bearing in mind however that these procedures are in no way units of signification such as a subsequent analysis of a semantic kind may one day manage to define; they are not strictly speaking part of the photographic structure. The procedures in question are familiar and no more will be attempted here than to translate them into structural terms. To be fully exact, the first three (trick effects, pose, objects) should be distinguished from the last three (photogenia, aestheticism, syntax), since in the former the connotation is produced by a modification of the reality itself, of, that is, the denoted message (such preparation is obviously not peculiar to the photograph). If they are nevertheless included amongst the connotation procedures, it is because they too benefit from the prestige of the denotation: the photograph allows the photographer to *conceal elusively* the preparation to which he subjects the scene to be recorded. Yet the fact still remains that there is no certainty from the point of view of a subsequent structural analysis that it will be possible to take into account the material they provide.

1. *Trick effects*. A photograph given wide circulation in the American press in 1951 is reputed to have cost Senator Millard Tydings his seat; it showed the Senator in conversation with the Communist leader Earl Browder. In fact, the photograph had been faked, created by the artificial bringing together of the two faces. The methodological interest of trick effects is that they intervene without warning in the plane of denotation; they utilize the special credibility of the photograph – this, as was seen, being simply its exceptional power of denotation – in order to pass off as merely denoted a message which is in reality heavily connoted; in no other treatment does connotation assume so completely the 'objective' mask of denotation. Naturally, signification is only possible to the extent that there is a stock of signs, the beginnings of a code. The signifier here is the conversational attitude of the two figures and it will be noted that this attitude becomes a sign only for a certain society, only given certain values. What makes the speakers' attitude the sign of a reprehensible familiarity is the tetchy anti-Communism of the American electorate; which is to say

that the code of connotation is neither artificial (as in a true language) nor natural, but historical.

2. *Pose*. Consider a press photograph of President Kennedy widely distributed at the time of the 1960 election: a half-length profile shot, eyes looking upwards, hands joined together. Here it is the very pose of the subject which prepares the reading of the signifieds of connotation: youthfulness, spirituality, purity. The photograph clearly only signifies because of the existence of a store of stereotyped attitudes which form ready-made elements of signification (eyes raised heavenwards, hands clasped). A 'historical grammar' of iconographic connotation ought thus to look for its material in painting, theatre, associations of ideas, stock metaphors, etc., that is to say, precisely in 'culture'. As has been said, pose is not a specifically photographic procedure but it is difficult not to mention it insofar as it derives its effect from the analogical principle at the basis of the photograph. The message in the present instance is not 'the pose' but 'Kennedy praying': the reader receives as a simple denotation what is in actual fact a double structure – denoted-connoted.

3. *Objects*. Special importance must be accorded to what could be called the posing of objects, where the meaning comes from the objects photographed (either because these objects have, if the photographer had the time, been artificially arranged in front of the camera or because the person responsible for lay-out chooses a photograph of this or that object). The interest lies in the fact that the objects are accepted inducers of associations of ideas (book-case = intellectual) or, in a more obscure way, are veritable symbols (the door of the gas-chamber for Chessman's execution with its reference to the funeral gates of ancient mythologies). Such objects constitute excellent elements of signification: on the one hand they are discontinuous and complete in themselves, a physical qualification for a sign, while on the

other they refer to clear, familiar signifieds. They are thus the elements of a veritable lexicon, stable to a degree which allows them to be readily constituted into syntax. Here, for example, is a 'composition' of objects: a window opening on to vineyards and tiled roofs; in front of the window a photograph album, a magnifying glass, a vase of flowers. Consequently, we are in the country, south of the Loire (vines and tiles), in a bourgeois house (flowers on the table) whose owner, advanced in years (the magnifying glass), is reliving his memories (the photograph album) – François Mauriac in Malagar (photo in *Paris-Match*). The connotation somehow 'emerges' from all these signifying units which are nevertheless 'captured' as though the scene were immediate and spontaneous, that is to say, without signification. The text renders the connotation explicit, developing the theme of Mauriac's ties with the land. Objects no longer perhaps possess a *power*, but they certainly possess meanings.

4. *Photogenia*. The theory of photogenia has already been developed (by Edgar Morin in *Le Cinéma ou l'homme imaginaire*[1]) and this is not the place to take up again the subject of the general signification of that procedure; it will suffice to define photogenia in terms of informational structure. In photogenia the connoted message is the image itself, 'embellished' (which is to say in general sublimated) by techniques of lighting, exposure and printing. An inventory needs to be made of these techniques, but only insofar as each of them has a corresponding signified of connotation sufficiently constant to allow its incorporation in a cultural lexicon of technical 'effects' (as for instance the 'blurring of movement' or 'flowingness' launched by Dr Steinert and his team to signify space-time). Such an inventory would be an excellent opportunity for distinguishing aesthetic effects from signifying effects – unless perhaps it be recognized that in photography, contrary to the intentions of

1. [Edgar Morin, *Le Cinéma ou l'homme imaginaire*, Paris 1956.]

exhibition photographers, there is never *art* but always *meaning*; which precisely would at last provide an exact criterion for the opposition between good painting, even if strongly representational, and photography.

5. *Aestheticism*. For if one can talk of aestheticism in photography, it is seemingly in an ambiguous fashion: when photography turns painting, composition or visual substance treated with deliberation in its very material 'texture', it is either so as to signify itself as 'art' (which was the case with the 'pictorialism' of the beginning of the century) or to impose a generally more subtle and complex signified than would be possible with other connotation procedures. Thus Cartier-Bresson constructed Cardinal Pacelli's reception by the faithful of Lisieux like a painting by an early master. The resulting photograph, however, is in no way a painting: on the one hand, its display of aestheticism refers (damagingly) to the very idea of a painting (which is contrary to any true painting); while on the other, the composition signifies in a declared manner a certain ecstatic spirituality translated precisely in terms of an objective spectacle. One can see here the difference between photograph and painting: in a picture by a Primitive, 'spirituality' is not a signified but, as it were, the very being of the image. Certainly there may be coded elements in some paintings, rhetorical figures, period symbols, but no signifying unit refers to spirituality, which is a mode of being and not the object of a structured message.

6. *Syntax*. We have already considered a discursive reading of object-signs within a single photograph. Naturally, several photographs can come together to form a sequence (this is commonly the case in illustrated magazines); the signifier of connotation is then no longer to be found at the level of any one of the fragments of the sequence but at that – what the linguists would call the suprasegmental level – of the concatenation. Consider for example

four snaps of a presidential shoot at Rambouillet: in each, the illustrious sportsman (Vincent Auriol) is pointing his rifle in some unlikely direction, to the great peril of the keepers who run away or fling themselves to the ground. The sequence (and the sequence alone) offers an effect of comedy which emerges, according to a familiar procedure, from the repetition and variation of the attitudes. It can be noted in this connection that the single photograph, contrary to the drawing, is very rarely (that is, only with much difficulty) comic; the comic requires movement, which is to say repetition (easy in film) or typification (possible in drawing), both these 'connotations' being prohibited to the photograph.

Text and image

Such are the main connotation procedures of the photographic image (once again, it is a question of techniques, not of units). To these may invariably be added the text which accompanies the press photograph. Three remarks should be made in this context.

Firstly, the text constitutes a parasitic message designed to connote the image, to 'quicken' it with one or more second-order signifieds. In other words, and this is an important historical reversal, the image no longer *illustrates* the words; it is now the words which, structurally, are parasitic on the image. The reversal is at a cost: in the traditional modes of illustration the image functioned as an episodic return to denotation from a principal message (the text) which was experienced as connoted since, precisely, it needed an illustration; in the relationship that now holds, it is not the image which comes to elucidate or 'realize' the text, but the latter which comes to sublimate, patheticize or rationalize the image. As however this operation is carried out accessorily, the new informational totality appears to be chiefly founded on an objective (denoted) message in relation to which the text is only a kind of secondary vibration, almost without consequence. Formerly, the image illustrated the text (made it clearer); today, the text loads the image, burdening it with a culture, a moral, an imagination. Formerly, there was reduction from text to image; today, there is amplification from the one to the other. The connotation is now experienced only as the natural resonance of the fundamental denotation constituted by the photographic analogy and we are thus confronted with a typical process of naturalization of the cultural.

Secondly, the effect of connotation probably differs according to the way in which the text is presented. The closer the text to the image, the less it seems to connote it; caught as it were in the iconographic message, the verbal message seems to share in its objectivity, the connotation of language is 'innocented' through the photograph's denotation. It is true that there is never a real incorporation since the substances of the two structures (graphic and iconic) are irreducible, but there are most likely degrees of amalgamation. The caption probably has a less obvious effect of connotation than the headline or accompanying article: headline and article are palpably separate from the image, the former by its emphasis, the latter by its distance; the first because it breaks, the other because it distances the content of the image. The caption, on the contrary, by its very disposition, by its average measure of reading, appears to duplicate the image, that is, to be included in its denotation.

It is impossible however (and this will be the final remark here concerning the text) that the words 'duplicate' the image; in the movement from one structure to the other second signifieds are inevitably developed. What is the relationship of these signifieds of connotation to the image? To all appearances, it is one of making explicit, of providing a stress; the text most often simply amplifying a set of connotations already given in the photograph. Sometimes, however, the text produces (invents) an entirely new signified which is retroactively projected into the image, so much so as to appear denoted there. '*They were near to death, their faces prove it*', reads the headline to a photograph showing Elizabeth and Philip leaving a plane – but at the moment of the photograph the two still knew nothing of the accident they had just escaped. Sometimes too, the text can even contradict the image so as to produce a compensatory connotation. An analysis by Gerbner (*The Social Anatomy of the Romance Confession Cover-girl*) demonstrated that in certain romance magazines the verbal message of the headlines, gloomy and anguished, on the cover always accompanied the image of a radiant cover-girl; here the two messages enter into a compromise, the connotation having a regulating function, preserving the irrational movement of projection-identification.

Photographic insignificance

We saw that the code of connotation was in all likelihood neither 'natural' nor 'artificial' but historical, or, if it be preferred, 'cultural'. Its signs are gestures, attitudes, expressions, colours or effects, endowed with certain meanings by virtue of the practice of a certain society: the link between signifier and signified remains if not unmotivated, at least entirely historical. Hence it is wrong to say that modern man projects into reading photographs feelings and values which are characterial or 'eternal' (infra- or trans-historical), unless it be firmly specified that *signification* is always developed by a given society and history. Signification, in short, is the dialectical movement which resolves the contradiction between cultural and natural man.

Thanks to its code of connotation the reading of the photograph is thus always historical; it depends on the reader's 'knowledge' just as though it were a matter of a real language [*langue*], intelligible only if one has learned the signs. All things considered, the photographic 'language' ['*langage*'] is not unlike certain ideographic languages which mix analogical and specifying units, the difference being that the ideogram is experienced as a sign whereas the photographic 'copy' is taken as the pure and simple denotation of reality. To find this code of connotation would thus be to isolate, inventoriate and structure all the 'historical' elements of the photograph, all the parts of the photographic surface which derive their very discontinuity from a certain knowledge on the reader's part, or, if one prefers, from the reader's cultural situation.

This task will perhaps take us a very long way indeed. Nothing tells us that the photograph contains 'neutral' parts, or at least it may be that complete insignificance in the photograph is quite exceptional. To resolve the problem, we would first of all need to elucidate fully the mechanisms of reading (in the physical, and no longer the semantic, sense of the term), of the perception of the photograph. But on this point we know very little. How do we read a photograph? What do we perceive? In what order, according to what progression? If, as is suggested by certain hypotheses of Bruner and Piaget, there is no perception without immediate categorization, then the photograph is verbalized in the very moment it is perceived; better, it is only perceived verbalized (if there is a delay in verbalization, there is disorder in perception, questioning, anguish for the subject, traumatism, following G. Cohen-Séat's hypothesis with regard to filmic perception). From this point of view, the image – grasped immediately by an inner metalanguage,

language itself – in actual fact has no denoted state, is immersed for its very social existence in at least an initial layer of connotation, that of the categories of language. We know that every language takes up a position with regard to things, that it connotes reality, if only in dividing it up; the connotations of the photograph would thus coincide, *grosso modo*, with the overall connotative planes of language.

In addition to 'perceptive' connotation, hypothetical but possible, one then encounters other, more particular, modes of connotation, and firstly a 'cognitive' connotation whose signifiers are picked out, localized, in certain parts of the analogon. Faced with such and such a townscape, I *know* that this is a North African country because on the left I can see a sign in Arabic script, in the centre a man wearing a gandoura, and so on. Here the reading closely depends on my culture, on my knowledge of the world, and it is probable that a good press photograph (and they are all good, being selected) makes ready play with the supposed knowledge of its readers, those prints being chosen which comprise the greatest possible quantity of information of this kind in such a way as to render the reading fully satisfying. If one photographs Agadir in ruins, it is better to have a few signs of 'Arabness' at one's disposal, even though 'Arabness' has nothing to do with the disaster itself; connotation drawn from knowledge is always a reassuring force – man likes signs and likes them clear.

Perceptive connotation, cognitive connotation; there remains the problem of ideological (in the very wide sense of the term) or ethical connotation, that which introduces reasons or values into the reading of the image. This is a strong connotation requiring a highly elaborated signifier of a readily syntactical order: conjunction of people (as was seen in the discussion of trick effects), development of attitudes, constellation of objects. A son has just been born to the Shah of Iran and in a photograph we have:

royalty (cot worshipped by a crowd of servants gathering round), wealth (several nursemaids), hygiene (white coats, cot covered in Plexiglass), the nevertheless human condition of kings (the baby is crying) – all the elements, that is, of the myth of princely birth as it is consumed today. In this instance the values are apolitical and their lexicon is abundant and clear. It is possible (but this is only a hypothesis) that political connotation is generally entrusted to the text, insofar as political choices are always, as it were, in bad faith: for a particular photograph I can give a right-wing reading or a left-wing reading (see in this connection an IFOP survey published by *Les Temps modernes* in 1955). Denotation, or the appearance of denotation, is powerless to alter political opinions: no photograph has ever convinced or refuted anyone (but the photograph can 'confirm') insofar as political consciousness is perhaps non-existent outside the *logos*: politics is what allows *all* languages.

These few remarks sketch a kind of differential table of photographic connotations, showing, if nothing else, that connotation extends a long way. Is this to say that a pure denotation, a *this-side of language*, is impossible? If such a denotation exists, it is perhaps not at the level of what ordinary language calls the insignificant, the neutral, the objective, but, on the contrary, at the level of absolutely traumatic images. The trauma is a suspension of language, a blocking of meaning. Certainly situations which are normally traumatic can be seized in a process of photographic signification but then precisely they are indicated via a rhetorical code which distances, sublimates and pacifies them. Truly traumatic photographs are rare, for in photography the trauma is wholly dependent on the certainty that the scene 'really' happened: *the photographer had to be there* (the mythical definition of denotation). Assuming this (which, in fact, is already a connotation), the traumatic photograph (fires, shipwrecks, catastrophes, violent deaths, all captured 'from life as lived') is the photograph about which there is nothing to say; the shock-photo is by structure insignificant: no value, no knowledge, at the limit no verbal categorization can have a hold on the process instituting the signification. One could imagine a kind of law: the more direct the trauma, the more difficult is connotation; or again, the 'mythological' effect of a photograph is inversely proportional to its traumatic effect.

Why? Doubtless because photographic connotation, like every well structured signification, is an institutional activity; in relation to society overall, its function is to integrate man, to reassure him. Every code is at once arbitrary and rational; recourse to a code is thus always an opportunity for man to prove himself, to test himself through a reason and a liberty. In this sense, the analysis of codes perhaps allows an easier and surer historical definition of a society than the analysis of its signifieds, for the latter can often appear as trans-historical, belonging more to an anthropological base than to a proper history. Hegel gave a better definition of the ancient Greeks by outlining the manner in which they made nature signify than by describing the totality of their 'feelings and beliefs' on the subject. Similarly, we can perhaps do better than to take stock directly of the ideological contents of our age; by trying to reconstitute in its specific structure the code of connotation of a mode of communication as important as the press photograph we may hope to find, in their very subtlety, the forms our society uses to ensure its peace of mind and to grasp thereby the magnitude, the detours and the underlying function of that activity. The prospect is the more appealing in that, as was said at the beginning, it develops with regard to the photograph in the form of a paradox – that which makes of an inert object a language and which transforms the unculture of a 'mechanical' art into the most social of institutions.

Rhetoric of the Image

According to an ancient etymology, the word *image* should be linked to the root *imitari*. Thus we find ourselves immediately at the heart of the most important problem facing the semiology of images: can analogical representation (the 'copy') produce true systems of signs and not merely simple agglutinations of symbols? Is it possible to conceive of an analogical 'code' (as opposed to a digital one)? We know that linguists refuse the status of language to all communication by analogy – from the 'language' of bees to the 'language' of gesture – the moment such communications are not doubly articulated, are not founded on a combinatory system of digital units as phonemes are. Nor are linguists the only ones to be suspicious as to the linguistic nature of the image; general opinion too has a vague conception of the image as an area of resistance to meaning – this in the name of a certain mythical idea of Life: the image is re-presentation, which is to say ultimately resurrection, and, as we know, the intelligible is reputed antipathetic to lived experience. Thus from both sides the image is felt to be weak in respect of meaning: there are those who think that the image is an extremely rudimentary system in comparison with language and those who think that signification cannot exhaust the image's ineffable richness. Now even – and above all if – the image is in a certain manner the *limit* of meaning, it permits the consideration of a veritable ontology of the process of signification. How does meaning get into the image? Where does it end? And if it ends, what is there *beyond*? Such are the questions that I wish to raise by submitting the image to a spectral analysis of the messages it may contain. We will start by making it considerably easier for ourselves: we will only study the advertising image. Why? Because in advertising the signification of the image is undoubtedly intentional; the signifieds of the advertising message are formed *a priori* by certain attributes of the product and these signifieds have to be transmitted as clearly as possible. If the image contains signs, we can be sure that in advertising these signs are full, formed with a view to the optimum reading: the advertising image is *frank*, or at least emphatic.

The three messages

Here we have a Panzani advertisement: some packets of pasta, a tin, a sachet, some tomatoes, onions, peppers, a mushroom, all emerging from a half-open string bag, in yellows and greens on a red background.[1] Let us try to 'skim off' the different messages it contains.

The image immediately yields a first message whose substance is linguistic; its supports are the caption, which is marginal, and the labels, these being inserted into the natural disposition of the scene, '*en abyme*'. The code from which this message has been taken is none other than that of the French language; the only knowledge required to decipher it is a knowledge of writing and French. In fact, this message can itself be further broken down, for the sign *Panzani* gives not simply the name of the firm but also, by its assonance, an additional signified, that of 'Italianicity'. The linguistic message is thus twofold (at least in this particular image): denotational and connotational. Since, however, we have here only a single typical sign,[2] namely

1. The *description* of the photograph is given here with prudence, for it already constitutes a metalanguage. The reader is asked to refer to the reproduction (XVII).

2. By *typical sign* is meant the sign of a system insofar as it is

that of articulated (written) language, it will be counted as one message.

Putting aside the linguistic message, we are left with the pure image (even if the labels are part of it, anecdotally). This image straightaway provides a series of discontinuous signs. First (the order is unimportant as these signs are not linear), the idea that what we have in the scene represented is a return from the market. A signified which itself implies two euphoric values: that of the freshness of the products and that of the essentially domestic preparation for which they are destined. Its signifier is the half-open bag which lets the provisions spill out over the table, 'unpacked'. To read this first sign requires only a knowledge which is in some sort implanted as part of the habits of a very widespread culture where 'shopping around for oneself' is opposed to the hasty stocking up (preserves, refrigerators) of a more 'mechanical' civilization. A second sign is more or less equally evident; its signifier is the bringing together of the tomato, the pepper and the tricoloured hues (yellow, green, red) of the poster; its signified is Italy or rather *Italianicity*. This sign stands in a relation of redundancy with the connoted sign of the linguistic message (the Italian assonance of the name *Panzani*) and the knowledge it draws upon is already more particular; it is a specifically 'French' knowledge (an Italian would barely perceive the connotation of the name, no more probably than he would the Italianicity of tomato and pepper), based on a familiarity with certain tourist stereotypes. Continuing to explore the image (which is not to say that it is not entirely clear at the first glance), there is no difficulty in discovering at least two other signs: in the first, the serried collection of different objects transmits the idea of a total culinary service, on the one hand as though Panzani furnished everything necessary

adequately defined by its substance: the verbal sign, the iconic sign, the gestural sign are so many typical signs.

for a carefully balanced dish and on the other as though the concentrate in the tin were equivalent to the natural produce surrounding it; in the other sign, the composition of the image, evoking the memory of innumerable alimentary paintings, sends us to an aesthetic signified: the *'nature morte'* or, as it is better expressed in other languages, the 'still life'[1]; the knowledge on which this sign depends is heavily cultural. It might be suggested that, in addition to these four signs, there is a further information pointer, that which tells us that this is an advertisement and which arises both from the place of the image in the magazine and from the emphasis of the labels (not to mention the caption). This last information, however, is co-extensive with the scene; it eludes signification insofar as the advertising nature of the image is essentially functional: to utter something is not necessarily to declare *I am speaking*, except in a deliberately reflexive system such as literature.

Thus there are four signs for this image and we will assume that they form a coherent whole (for they are all discontinuous), require a generally cultural knowledge, and refer back to signifieds each of which is global (for example, *Italianicity*), imbued with euphoric values. After the linguistic message, then, we can see a second, iconic message. Is that the end? If all these signs are removed from the image, we are still left with a certain informational matter; deprived of all knowledge, I continue to 'read' the image, to 'understand' that it assembles in a common space a number of identifiable (nameable) objects, not merely shapes and colours. The signifieds of this third message are constituted by the real objects in the scene, the signifiers by these same objects photographed, for, given that the relation between thing signified and image signifying in analogical representation is not 'arbitrary' (as it is in lan-

1. In French, the expression *nature morte* refers to the original presence of funereal objects, such as a skull, in certain pictures.

guage), it is no longer necessary to dose the relay with a third term in the guise of the psychic image of the object. What defines the third message is precisely that the relation between signified and signifier is quasi-tautological; no doubt the photograph involves a certain arrangement of the scene (framing, reduction, flattening) but this transition is not a *transformation* (in the way a coding can be); we have here a loss of the equivalence characteristic of true sign systems and a statement of quasi-identity. In other words, the sign of this message is not drawn from an institutional stock, is not coded, and we are brought up against the paradox (to which we will return) of a *message without a code*.[1] This peculiarity can be seen again at the level of the knowledge invested in the reading of the message; in order to 'read' this last (or first) level of the image, all that is needed is the knowledge bound up with our perception. That knowledge is not nil, for we need to know what an image is (children only learn this at about the age of four) and what a tomato, a string-bag, a packet of pasta are, but it is a matter of an almost anthropological knowledge. This message corresponds, as it were, to the letter of the image and we can agree to call it the literal message, as opposed to the previous symbolic message.

If our reading is satisfactory, the photograph analysed offers us three messages: a linguistic message, a coded iconic message, and a non-coded iconic message. The linguistic message can be readily separated from the other two, but since the latter share the same (iconic) substance, to what extent have we the right to separate them? It is certain that the distinction between the two iconic messages is not made spontaneously in ordinary reading: the viewer of the image receives *at one and the same time* the perceptual message and the cultural message, and it will be seen later that this confusion in reading corresponds to the function

1. Cf. 'The photographic message', above pp. 15–31.

of the mass image (our concern here). The distinction, however, has an operational validity, analogous to that which allows the distinction in the linguistic sign of a signifier and a signified (even though in reality no one is able to separate the 'word' from its meaning except by recourse to the metalanguage of a definition). If the distinction permits us to describe the structure of the image in a simple and coherent fashion and if this description paves the way for an explanation of the role of the image in society, we will take it to be justified. The task now is thus to reconsider each type of message so as to explore it in its generality, without losing sight of our aim of understanding the overall structure of the image, the final inter-relationship of the three messages. Given that what is in question is not a 'naive' analysis but a structural description,[1] the order of the messages will be modified a little by the inversion of the cultural message and the literal message; of the two iconic messages, the first is in some sort imprinted on the second: the literal message appears as the *support* of the 'symbolic' message. Hence, knowing that a system which takes over the signs of another system in order to make them its signifiers is a system of connotation,[2] we may say immediately that the literal image is *denoted* and the symbolic image *connoted*. Successively, then, we shall look at the linguistic message, the denoted image, and the connoted image.

The linguistic message

Is the linguistic message constant? Is there always textual

1. 'Naive' analysis is an enumeration of elements, structural description aims to grasp the relation of these elements by virtue of the principle of the solidarity holding between the terms of a structure: if one term changes, so also do the others.
2. Cf. R. Barthes, *Eléments de sémiologie*, *Communications* 4, 1964, p. 130 [trans. *Elements of Semiology*, London 1967 & New York 1968, pp. 89–92].

matter in, under, or around the image? In order to find images given without words, it is doubtless necessary to go back to partially illiterate societies, to a sort of pictographic state of the image. From the moment of the appearance of the book, the linking of text and image is frequent, though it seems to have been little studied from a structural point of view. What is the signifying structure of 'illustration'? Does the image duplicate certain of the informations given in the text by a phenomenon of redundancy or does the text add a fresh information to the image? The problem could be posed historically as regards the classical period with its passion for books with pictures (it was inconceivable in the eighteenth century that editions of La Fontaine's *Fables* should not be illustrated) and its authors such as Menestrier who concerned themselves with the relations between figure and discourse.[1] Today, at the level of mass communications, it appears that the linguistic message is indeed present in every image: as title, caption, accompanying press article, film dialogue, comic strip balloon. Which shows that it is not very accurate to talk of a civilization of the image — we are still, and more than ever, a civilization of writing,[2] writing and speech continuing to be the full terms of the informational structure. In fact, it is simply the presence of the linguistic message that counts, for neither its position nor its length seem to be pertinent (a long text may only comprise a single global signified, thanks to connotation, and it is this signified which is put in relation with the image). What are the functions of the linguistic message with regard to the (twofold) iconic message? There appear to be two: *anchorage* and *relay*.

As will be seen more clearly in a moment, all images are

1. Menestrier, *L'Art des emblèmes*, 1684.
2. Images without words can certainly be found in certain cartoons, but by way of a paradox; the absence of words always covers an enigmatic intention.

polysemous; they imply, underlying their signifiers, a 'floating chain' of signifieds, the reader able to choose some and ignore others. Polysemy poses a question of meaning and this question always comes through as a dysfunction, even if this dysfunction is recuperated by society as a tragic (silent, God provides no possibility of choosing between signs) or a poetic (the panic 'shudder of meaning' of the Ancient Greeks) game; in the cinema itself, traumatic images are bound up with an uncertainty (an anxiety) concerning the meaning of objects or attitudes. Hence in every society various techniques are developed intended to *fix* the floating chain of signifieds in such a way as to counter the terror of uncertain signs; the linguistic message is one of these techniques. At the level of the literal message, the text replies – in a more or less direct, more or less partial manner – to the question: *what is it?* The text helps to identify purely and simply the elements of the scene and the scene itself; it is a matter of a denoted description of the image (a description which is often incomplete) or, in Hjelmslev's terminology, of an *operation* (as opposed to connotation).[1] The denominative function corresponds exactly to an *anchorage* of all the possible (denoted) meanings of the object by recourse to a nomenclature. Shown a plateful of something (in an *Amieux* advertisement), I may hesitate in identifying the forms and masses; the caption ('*rice and tuna fish with mushrooms*') helps me to choose *the correct level of perception*, permits me to focus not simply my gaze but also my understanding. When it comes to the 'symbolic message', the linguistic message no longer guides identification but interpretation, constituting a kind of vice which holds the connoted meanings from proliferating, whether towards excessively individual regions (it limits, that is to say, the projective power of the image) or towards dysphoric values. An advertisement (for *d'Arcy* preserves)

1. *Eléments de sémiologie*, pp. 131–2 [trans. pp. 90–4].

shows a few fruits scattered around a ladder; the caption ('*as if from your own garden*') banishes one possible signified (parsimony, the paucity of the harvest) because of its un-pleasantness and orientates the reading towards a more flattering signified (the natural and personal character of fruit from a private garden); it acts here as a counter-taboo, combatting the disagreeable myth of the artificial usually associated with preserves. Of course, elsewhere than in ad-vertising, the anchorage may be ideological and indeed this is its principal function; the text *directs* the reader through the signifieds of the image, causing him to avoid some and receive others; by means of an often subtle *dispatching*, it remote-controls him towards a meaning chosen in advance. In all these cases of anchorage, language clearly has a function of elucidation, but this elucidation is selec-tive, a metalanguage applied not to the totality of the iconic message but only to certain of its signs. The text is indeed the creator's (and hence society's) right of inspection over the image; anchorage is a control, bearing a responsibility – in the face of the projective power of pictures – for the use of the message. With respect to the liberty of the signifieds of the image, the text has thus a *repressive* value[1] and we can see that it is at this level that the morality and ideology of a society are above all invested.

Anchorage is the most frequent function of the linguistic

1. This can be seen clearly in the paradoxical case where the image is constructed according to the text and where, consequently, the control would seem to be needless. An advertisement which wants to com-municate that in such and such a coffee the aroma is 'locked in' the product in powder form and that it will thus be wholly there when the coffee is used depicts, above this proposition, a tin of coffee with a chain and padlock round it. Here, the linguistic metaphor ('locked in') is taken literally (a well-known poetic device); in fact, however, it is the image which is read first and the text from which the image is constructed becomes in the end the simple choice of one signified among others. The repression is present again in the circular movement as a banalization of the message.

message and is commonly found in press photographs and advertisements. The function of relay is less common (at least as far as the fixed image is concerned); it can be seen particularly in cartoons and comic strips. Here text (most often a snatch of dialogue) and image stand in a complementary relationship; the words, in the same way as the images, are fragments of a more general syntagm and the unity of the message is realized at a higher level, that of the story, the anecdote, the diegesis (which is ample confirmation that the diegesis must be treated as an autonomous system[1]). While rare in the fixed image, this relay-text becomes very important in film, where dialogue functions not simply as elucidation but really does advance the action by setting out, in the sequence of messages, meanings that are not to be found in the image itself. Obviously, the two functions of the linguistic message can co-exist in the one iconic whole, but the dominance of the one or the other is of consequence for the general economy of a work. When the text has the diegetic value of relay, the information is more costly, requiring as it does the learning of a digital code (the system of language); when it has a substitute value (anchorage, control), it is the image which detains the informational charge and, the image being analogical, the information is then 'lazier': in certain comic strips intended for 'quick' reading the diegesis is confided above all to the text, the image gathering the attributive informations of a paradigmatic order (the stereotyped status of the characters); the costly message and the discursive message are made to coincide so that the hurried reader may be spared the boredom of verbal 'descriptions', which are entrusted to the image, that is to say to a less 'laborious' system.

1. Cf. Claude Bremond, 'Le message narratif', *Communications* 4, 1964.

The denoted image

We have seen that in the image properly speaking, the distinction between the literal message and the symbolic message is operational; we never encounter (at least in advertising) a literal image in a pure state. Even if a totally 'naive' image were to be achieved, it would immediately join the sign of naivety and be completed by a third – symbolic – message. Thus the characteristics of the literal message cannot be substantial but only relational. It is first of all, so to speak, a message by eviction, constituted by what is left in the image when the signs of connotation are mentally deleted (it would not be possible actually to remove them for they can impregnate the whole of the image, as in the case of the 'still life composition'). This evictive state naturally corresponds to a plenitude of virtualities: it is an absence of meaning full of all the meanings. Then again (and there is no contradiction with what has just been said), it is a sufficient message, since it has at least one meaning at the level of the identification of the scene represented; the letter of the image corresponds in short to the first degree of intelligibility (below which the reader would perceive only lines, forms, and colours), but this intelligibility remains virtual by reason of its very poverty, for everyone from a real society always disposes of a knowledge superior to the merely anthropological and perceives more than just the letter. Since it is both evictive and sufficient, it will be understood that from an aesthetic point of view the denoted image can appear as a kind of Edenic state of the image; cleared utopianically of its connotations, the image would become radically objective, or, in the last analysis, innocent.

This utopian character of denotation is considerably reinforced by the paradox already mentioned, that the photograph (in its literal state), by virtue of its absolutely analogical nature, seems to constitute a message without a code. Here, however, structural analysis must differentiate, for of all the kinds of image only the photograph is able to transmit the (literal) information without forming it by means of discontinuous signs and rules of transformation. The photograph, message without a code, must thus be opposed to the drawing which, even when denoted, is a coded message. The coded nature of the drawing can be seen at three levels. Firstly, to reproduce an object or a scene in a drawing requires a set of *rule-governed* transpositions; there is no essential nature of the pictorial copy and the codes of transposition are historical (notably those concerning perspective). Secondly, the operation of the drawing (the coding) immediately necessitates a certain division between the significant and the insignificant: the drawing does not reproduce *everything* (often it reproduces very little), without its ceasing, however, to be a strong message; whereas the photograph, although it can choose its subject, its point of view and its angle, cannot intervene *within* the object (except by trick effects). In other words, the denotation of the drawing is less pure than that of the photograph, for there is no drawing without style. Finally, like all codes, the drawing demands an apprenticeship (Saussure attributed a great importance to this semiological fact). Does the coding of the denoted message have consequences for the connoted message? It is certain that the coding of the literal prepares and facilitates connotation since it at once establishes a certain discontinuity in the image: the 'execution' of a drawing itself constitutes a connotation. But at the same time, insofar as the drawing displays its coding, the relationship between the two messages is profoundly modified: it is no longer the relationship between a nature and a culture (as with the photograph) but that between two cultures; the 'ethic' of the drawing is not the same as that of the photograph.

In the photograph – at least at the level of the literal message – the relationship of signifieds to signifiers is not one of 'transformation' but of 'recording', and the absence of a code clearly reinforces the myth of photographic 'naturalness': the scene *is there*, captured mechanically, not humanly (the mechanical is here a guarantee of objectivity). Man's interventions in the photograph (framing, distance, lighting, focus, speed) all effectively belong to the plane of connotation; it is as though in the beginning (even if utopian) there were a brute photograph (frontal and clear) on which man would then lay out, with the aid of various techniques, the signs drawn from a cultural code. Only the opposition of the cultural code and the natural non-code can, it seems, account for the specific character of the photograph and allow the assessment of the anthropological revolution it represents in man's history. The type of consciousness the photograph involves is indeed truly unprecedented, since it establishes not a consciousness of the *being-there* of the thing (which any copy could provoke) but an awareness of its *having-been-there*. What we have is a new space-time category: spatial immediacy and temporal anteriority, the photograph being an illogical conjunction between the *here-now* and the *there-then*. It is thus at the level of this denoted message or message without code that the *real unreality* of the photograph can be fully understood: its unreality is that of the *here-now*, for the photograph is never experienced as illusion, is in no way a *presence* (claims as to the magical character of the photographic image must be deflated); its reality that of the *having-been-there*, for in every photograph there is the always stupefying evidence of *this is how it was*, giving us, by a precious miracle, a reality from which we are sheltered. This kind of temporal equilibrium (*having-been-there*) probably diminishes the projective power of the image (very few psychological tests resort to photographs while many use drawings): the *this was so* easily defeats the *it's me*. If these remarks are at all correct, the photograph must be related to a pure spectatorial consciousness and not to the more projective, more 'magical' fictional consciousness on which film by and large depends. This would lend authority to the view that the distinction between film and photograph is not a simple difference of degree but a radical opposition. Film can no longer be seen as animated photographs: the *having-been-there* gives way before a *being-there* of the thing; which omission would explain how there can be a history of the cinema, without any real break with the previous arts of fiction, whereas the photograph can in some sense elude history (despite the evolution of the techniques and ambitions of the photographic art) and represent a 'flat' anthropological fact, at once absolutely new and definitively unsurpassable, humanity encountering for the first time in its history *messages without a code*. Hence the photograph is not the last (improved) term of the great family of images; it corresponds to a decisive mutation of informational economies.

At all events, the denoted image, to the extent to which it does not imply any code (the case with the advertising photograph), plays a special role in the general structure of the iconic message which we can begin to define (returning to this question after discussion of the third message): the denoted image naturalizes the symbolic message, it innocents the semantic artifice of connotation, which is extremely dense, especially in advertising. Although the *Panzani* poster is full of 'symbols', there nonetheless remains in the photograph, insofar as the literal message is sufficient, a kind of natural *being-there* of objects: nature seems spontaneously to produce the scene represented. A pseudo-truth is surreptitiously substituted for the simple validity of openly semantic systems; the absence of code disintellectualizes the message because it seems to found in nature the signs of culture. This is without doubt an important historical paradox: the more technology develops the diffusion of information (and notably of images), the more it provides the means of masking the constructed meaning under the appearance of the given meaning.

Rhetoric of the image

It was seen that the signs of the third message (the 'symbolic' message, cultural or connoted) were discontinuous. Even when the signifier seems to extend over the whole image, it is nonetheless a sign separated from the others: the 'composition' carries an aesthetic signified, in much the same way as intonation although suprasegmental is a separate signifier in language. Thus we are here dealing with a normal system whose signs are drawn from a cultural code (even if the linking together of the elements of the sign appears more or less analogical). What gives this system its originality is that the number of readings of the same lexical unit or *lexia* (of the same image) varies according to individuals. In the *Panzani* advertisement analysed, four connotative signs have been identified; probably there are others (the net bag, for example, can signify the miraculous draught of fishes, plenty, etc.). The variation in readings is not, however, anarchic; it depends on the different kinds of knowledge – practical, national, cultural, aesthetic – invested in the image and these can be classified, brought into a typology. It is as though the image presented itself to the reading of several different people who can perfectly well co-exist in a single individual: *the one lexia mobilizes different lexicons*. What is a lexicon? A portion of the symbolic plane (of language) which corresponds to a body of practices and techniques.[1] This is the case for the different

1. Cf. A. J. Greimas, 'Les problèmes de la description mécano-graphique', *Cahiers de Lexicologie*, 1, 1959, p. 63.

readings of the image: each sign corresponds to a body of 'attitudes' – tourism, housekeeping, knowledge of art – certain of which may obviously be lacking in this or that individual. There is a plurality and a co-existence of lexicons in one and the same person, the number and identity of these lexicons forming in some sort a person's *idiolect*.[1] The image, in its connotation, is thus constituted by an architecture of signs drawn from a variable depth of lexicons (of idiolects); each lexicon, no matter how 'deep', still being coded, if, as is thought today, the *psyche* itself is articulated like a language; indeed, the further one 'descends' into the psychic depths of an individual, the more rarified and the more classifiable the signs become – what could be more systematic than the readings of Rorschach tests? The variability of readings, therefore, is no threat to the 'language' of the image if it be admitted that that language is composed of idiolects, lexicons and sub-codes. The image is penetrated through and through by the system of meaning, in exactly the same way as man is articulated to the very depths of his being in distinct languages. The language of the image is not merely the totality of utterances emitted (for example at the level of the combiner of the signs or creator of the message), it is also the totality of utterances received:[2] the language must include the 'surprises' of meaning.

Another difficulty in analysing connotation is that there is no particular analytical language corresponding to the particularity of its signifieds – how are the signifieds of connotation to be named? For one of them we ventured the term *Italianicity*, but the others can only be designated

1. Cf. *Eléments de sémiologie*, p. 96 [trans. pp. 21–2].
2. In the Saussurian perspective, speech (utterances) is above all that which is emitted, drawn from the language-system (and constituting it in return). It is necessary today to enlarge the notion of language [*langue*], especially from the semantic point of view: language is the 'totalizing abstraction' of the messages emitted *and received*.

by words from ordinary language (*culinary preparation*, *still life*, *plenty*); the metalanguage which has to take charge of them at the moment of the analysis is not specialized. This is a difficulty, for these signifieds have a particular semantic nature; as a seme of connotation, 'plenty' does not exactly cover 'plenty' in the denoted sense; the signifier of connotation (here the profusion and the condensation of the produce) is like the essential cipher of all possible plenties, of the purest idea of plenty. The denoted word never refers to an essence for it is always caught up in a contingent utterance, a continuous syntagm (that of verbal discourse), oriented towards a certain practical transitivity of language; the seme 'plenty', on the contrary, is a concept in a pure state, cut off from any syntagm, deprived of any context and corresponding to a sort of theatrical state of meaning, or, better (since it is a question of a sign without a syntagm), to an *exposed* meaning. To express these semes of connotation would therefore require a special metalanguage and we are left with barbarisms of the *Italianicity* kind as best being able to account for the signifieds of connotation, the suffix -*icity* deriving an abstract noun from the adjective: *Italianicity* is not Italy, it is the condensed essence of everything that could be Italian, from spaghetti to painting. By accepting to regulate artificially – and if needs be barbarously – the naming of the semes of connotation, the analysis of their form will be rendered easier.[1] These semes are organized in associative fields, in paradigmatic articulations, even perhaps in oppositions, according to certain defined paths or, as A. J. Greimas puts it, according to certain semic axes:[2] *Italianicity* belongs to a certain axis of nationalities, alongside Frenchicity, Germanicity or

1. *Form* in the precise sense given it by Hjelmslev (cf. *Eléments de sémiologie*, p. 105 [trans. pp. 39–41]), as the functional organization of the signifieds among themselves.

2. A. J. Greimas, *Cours de Sémantique*, 1964 (notes roneotyped by he Ecole Normale Supérieure de Saint-Cloud).

Spanishicity. The reconstitution of such axes – which may eventually be in opposition to one another – will clearly only be possible once a massive inventory of the systems of connotation has been carried out, an inventory not merely of the connotative system of the image but also of those of other substances, for if connotation has typical signifiers dependent on the different substances utilized (image, language, objects, modes of behaviour) it holds all its signifieds in common: the same signifieds are to be found in the written press, the image or the actor's gestures (which is why semiology can only be conceived in a so to speak total framework). This common domain of the signifieds of connotation is that of *ideology*, which cannot but be single for a given society and history, no matter what signifiers of connotation it may use.

To the general ideology, that is, correspond signifiers of connotation which are specified according to the chosen substance. These signifiers will be called *connotators* and the set of connotators a *rhetoric*, rhetoric thus appearing as the signifying aspect of ideology. Rhetorics inevitably vary by their substance (here articulated sound, there image, gesture or whatever) but not necessarily by their form; it is even probable that there exists a single rhetorical *form*, common for instance to dream, literature and image.[1] Thus the rhetoric of the image (that is to say, the classification of its connotators) is specific to the extent that it is subject to the physical constraints of vision (different, for example, from phonatory constraints) but general to the extent that the 'figures' are never more than formal relations of elements. This rhetoric could only be established on the basis of a quite considerable inventory, but it is

1. Cf. Emile Benveniste, 'Remarques sur la fonction du langage dans la découverte freudienne', *La Psychanalyse* 1, 1956, pp. 3–16 [reprinted in E. Benveniste, *Problèmes de linguistique générale*, Paris 1966, Chapter 7; translated as *Problems of General Linguistics*, Coral Gables, Florida 1971].

possible now to foresee that one will find in it some of the figures formerly identified by the Ancients and the Classics;[1] the tomato, for example, signifies *Italianicity* by metonymy and in another advertisement the sequence of three scenes (coffee in beans, coffee in powder, coffee sipped in the cup) releases a certain logical relationship in the same way as an asyndeton. It is probable indeed that among the meta-bolas (or figures of the substitution of one signifier for another[2]), it is metonymy which furnishes the image with the greatest number of its connotators, and that among the parataxes (or syntagmatic figures), it is asyndeton which predominates.

The most important thing, however, at least for the moment, is not to inventorize the connotators but to understand that in the total image they constitute *dis-continuous* or better still *scattered traits*. The connotators do not fill the whole of the lexia, reading them does not exhaust it. In other words (and this would be a valid pro-position for semiology in general), not all the elements of the lexia can be transformed into connotators; there always remaining in the discourse a certain denotation without which, precisely, the discourse would not be possible. Which brings us back to the second message or denoted image. In the *Panzani* advertisement, the Mediterranean vegetables, the colour, the composition, the very profusion rise up as so many scattered blocks, at once isolated and mounted in a general scene which has its own space and, as was seen, its 'meaning': they are 'set' in a syntagm *which*

1. Classical rhetoric needs to be rethought in structural terms (this is the object of a work in progress); it will then perhaps be possible to establish a general rhetoric or linguistics of the signifiers of connota-tion, valid for articulated sound, image, gesture, etc. See 'L'ancienne Rhétorique (Aide-mémoire)', *Communications* 16, 1970.

2. We prefer here to evade Jakobson's opposition between metaphor and metonymy for if metonymy by its origin is a figure of contiguity, it nevertheless functions finally as a substitute of the signifier, that is as a metaphor.

is not theirs and which is that of the denotation. This last proposition is important for it permits us to found (retroactively) the structural distinction between the second or literal message and the third or symbolic message and to give a more exact description of the naturalizing function of the denotation with respect to the connotation. We can now understand that *it is precisely the syntagm of the denoted message which 'naturalizes' the system of the connoted message.* Or again: connotation is only system, can only be defined in paradigmatic terms; iconic denotation is only syntagm, associates elements without any system: the discontinuous connotators are connected, actualized, 'spoken' through the syntagm of the denotation, the discontinuous world of symbols plunges into the story of the denoted scene as though into a lustral bath of innocence.

It can thus be seen that in the total system of the image the structural functions are polarized: on the one hand there is a sort of paradigmatic condensation at the level of the connotators (that is, broadly speaking, of the symbols), which are strong signs, scattered, 'reified'; on the other a syntagmatic 'flow' at the level of the denotation – it will not be forgotten that the syntagm is always very close to speech, and it is indeed the iconic 'discourse' which naturalizes its symbols. Without wishing to infer too quickly from the image to semiology in general, one can nevertheless venture that the world of total meaning is torn internally (structurally) between the system as culture and the syntagm as nature: the works of mass communications all combine, through diverse and diversely successful dialectics, the fascination of a nature, that of story, diegesis, syntagm, and the intelligibility of a culture, withdrawn into a few discontinuous symbols which men 'decline' in the shelter of their living speech.

The Third Meaning

Research notes on some Eisenstein stills

For Nordine Saïl, director of Cinema 3

Here is an image from *Ivan the Terrible* (I): two courtiers, two adjuvants, two supernumeraries (it matters little if I am unable to remember the details of the story exactly) are raining down gold over the young czar's head. I think it possible to distinguish three levels of meaning in this scene:

1) An informational level, which gathers together everything I can learn from the setting, the costumes, the characters, their relations, their insertion in an anecdote with which I am (even if vaguely) familiar. This level is that of communication. Were it necessary to find a mode of analysis for it, I should turn to the first semiotics (that of the 'message'); this level, this semiotics, however, will be of no further concern here.

2) A symbolic level, which is the downpour of gold and which is itself stratified. There is the referential symbolism: the imperial ritual of baptism by gold. Then there is the diegetic symbolism: the theme of gold, of wealth, in *Ivan the Terrible* (supposing such a theme to exist), which makes a significant intervention in this scene. Then again there is the Eisensteinian symbolism – if by chance a critic should decide to demonstrate that the gold or the raining down or the curtain or the disfiguration can be seen as held in a network of displacements and substitutions peculiar to S. M. Eisenstein. Finally, there is an historical symbolism, if, in a manner even more widely embracing than the previous ones, it can be shown that the gold brings in a (theatrical) playing, a scenography of exchange, locatable both psychoanalytically and economically, that is to say semiologically. Taken in its entirety, this second level is that of *signification*.

Its mode of analysis would be a semiotics more highly developed than the first, a second or neo-semiotics, open no longer to the science of the message but to the sciences of the symbol (psychoanalysis, economy, dramaturgy).

3) Is that all? No, for I am still held by the image. I read, I receive (and probably even first and foremost) a third meaning[1] – evident, erratic, obstinate. I do not know what its signified is, at least I am unable to give it a name, but I can see clearly the traits, the signifying accidents of which this – consequently incomplete – sign is composed: a certain compactness of the courtiers' make-up, thick and insistent for the one, smooth and distinguished for the other; the former's 'stupid' nose, the latter's finely traced eyebrows, his lank blondness, his faded, pale complexion, the affected flatness of his hairstyle suggestive of a wig, the touching-up with chalky foundation talc, with face powder. I am not sure if the reading of this third meaning is justified – if it can be generalized – but already it seems to me that its signifier (the traits to which I have tried to give words, if not to describe) possesses a theoretical individuality. On the one hand, it cannot be conflated with the simple *existence* of the scene, it exceeds the copy of the referential motif, it compels an interrogative reading (interrogation bears precisely on the signifier not on the signified, on reading not on intellection: it is a 'poetical' grasp); on the other, neither can it be conflated with the dramatic meaning of the episode: to say that these traits refer to a significant 'attitude' of the courtiers, this one detached and bored, that one diligent (*'They are simply doing their job as courtiers'*),

1. In the classical paradigm of the five senses, the third sense is hearing (first in importance in the Middle Ages). This is a happy coincidence, since what is here in question is indeed *listening*: firstly, because the remarks by Eisenstein to which reference will be made are taken from a consideration of the coming of sound in film; second, because listening (no reference to the *phoné* alone) bears within it that metaphor best suited to the 'textual': orchestration (SME's own word), counterpoint, stereophony.

does not leave me fully satisfied; something in the two faces exceeds psychology, anecdote, function, exceeds meaning without, however, coming down to the obstinacy in presence shown by any human body. By contrast with the first two levels, communication and signification, this third level – even if the reading of it is still hazardous – is that of *signifiance*, a word which has the advantage of referring to the field of the signifier (and not of signification) and of linking up with, via the path opened by Julia Kristeva who proposed the term, a semiotics of the text.

My concern here lies not with communication but with signification and *signifiance*. I must therefore name as economically as possible the second and third meanings. The symbolic meaning (the shower of gold, the power of wealth, the imperial rite) forces itself upon me by a double determination: it is intentional (it is what the author wanted to say) and it is taken from a kind of common, general lexicon of symbols; it is a meaning which seeks me out, me, the recipient of the message, the subject of the reading, a meaning which starts with SME and which goes on *ahead of me;* evident certainly (so too is the other), but *closed* in its evidence, held in a complete system of destination. I propose to call this complete sign *the obvious meaning*. *Obvius* means *which comes ahead* and this is exactly the case with this meaning, which comes to seek me out. In theology, we are told, the obvious meaning is that 'which presents itself quite naturally to the mind' and this again is the case here: the symbolics of the raining down of gold appears to me as for ever having been endowed with a 'natural' clarity. As for the other meaning, the third, the one 'too many', the supplement that my intellection cannot succeed in absorbing, at once persistent and fleeting, smooth and elusive, I propose to call it *the obtuse meaning*. The word springs readily to mind and, miracle, when its etymology is unfolded, it already provides us with a theory of the supplementary meaning. *Obtusus* means *that which is blunted, rounded in form*. Are not the traits which I indicated (the make-up, the whiteness, the wig, etc.) just like the blunting of a meaning too clear, too violent? Do they not give the obvious signified a kind of difficultly prehensible roundness, cause my reading to slip? An obtuse angle is greater than a right angle: *an obtuse angle of 100°*, says the dictionary; the third meaning also seems to me greater than the pure, upright, secant, legal perpendicular of the narrative, it seems to open the field of meaning totally, that is infinitely. I even accept for the obtuse meaning the word's pejorative connotation: the obtuse meaning appears to extend outside culture, knowledge, information; analytically, it has something derisory about it: opening out into the infinity of language, it can come through as limited in the eyes of analytic reason; it belongs to the family of pun, buffoonery, useless expenditure. Indifferent to moral or aesthetic categories (the trivial, the futile, the false, the pastiche), it is on the side of the carnival. *Obtuse* is thus very suitable.

The obvious meaning

A few words with regard to the obvious meaning, even though it is not the object of this study. Here are two images in which it can be seen in its pure state. The four figures in II 'symbolize' three ages of life and the unanimity of mourning (Vakulinchuk's funeral). The clenched fist in IV, given in full 'detail', signifies indignation, anger mastered and channelled, the determination of the struggle; metonymically joined to the whole Potemkin story, it 'symbolizes' the working class in all its resolute strength, for, by a miracle of semantic intelligence, this fist which is *seen wrong way up*, kept by its owner in a sort of clandestinity (it is the hand which *first of all* hangs down naturally along the trouser leg and which *then* closes, hardens, *thinks* at once its future struggle, its patience and its prudence), cannot be read as the fist of some hoodlum, of some fascist: it is *immediately* a proletarian fist. Which shows that Eisenstein's 'art' is not polysemous: it chooses the meaning, imposes it, hammers it home (if the signification is overrun by the obtuse meaning, this is not to say that it is thereby denied or blurred): the Eisensteinian meaning devastates ambiguity. How? By the addition of an aesthetic value, emphasis. Eisenstein's 'decorativism' has an economic function: it proffers the truth. Look at III: in extremely classic fashion, grief comes from the bowed heads, the expressions of suffering, the hand over the mouth stifling a sob, but when once all this has been said, very adequately, a decorative trait says it again: the superimposition of the two hands aesthetically arranged in a delicate, maternal, floral ascension towards the face bowing down. Within the general detail (the two women), another detail is mirroringly inscribed; derived from a pictorial order as a quotation of the gestures to be found in icons and *pietà*, it does not distract but accentuates the meaning. This accentuation (characteristic of all realist art) has some connection with the 'truth' of *Potemkin*. Baudelaire spoke of '*the emphatic truth of gesture in the important moments of life*'; here it is the truth of the 'important proletarian moment' which requires emphasis. The Eisensteinian aesthetic does not constitute an independent level: it is part of the obvious meaning, and the obvious meaning is always, in Eisenstein, the revolution.

The obtuse meaning

I first had the conviction of the obtuse meaning with image V. A question forced itself upon me: what is it in this tearful old woman that poses for me the question of the signifier? I quickly convinced myself that, although perfect, it was neither the facial expression nor the gestural figuration of grief (the closed eyelids, the taut mouth, the hand clasped on the breast): all that belongs to the full signification, to the obvious meaning of the image, to Eisensteinian realism and decorativism. I felt that the penetrating trait – disturbing like a guest who obstinately sits on saying nothing when one has no use for him – must be situated somewhere in the region of the forehead: the coif, the headscarf holding in the hair, had something to do with it. In image VI, however, the obtuse meaning vanishes, leaving only a message of grief. It was then I understood that the scandal, supplement or drift imposed on this classic representation of grief came very precisely from a tenuous relationship: that of the low headscarf, the closed eyes and the convex mouth; or rather, to use the distinction made by SME himself between 'the shadows of the cathedral' and 'the enshadowed cathedral', from a relation between the 'lowness' of the line of the headscarf, pulled down abnormally close to the eyebrows as in those disguises intended to create a facetious, simpleton look, the upward circumflex of the faded eyebrows, faint and old, the excessive curve of the eyelids, lowered but brought together as though squinting, and the bar of the half-opened mouth, corresponding to the bar of the headscarf and to that of the eyebrows, metaphorically speaking 'like a fish out of water'. All these traits (the funny headdress, the old woman, the squinting eyelids, the fish) have as their vague reference a somewhat low language, the language of a rather pitiful disguise. In connection with the noble grief of the obvious meaning, they form a dialogism so tenuous that there is no guarantee of its intentionality. The characteristic of this third meaning is indeed – at least in SME – to blur the limit separating expression from disguise, but also to allow that oscillation succinct demonstration – an elliptic emphasis, if one can put it like that, a complex and extremely artful disposition (for it involves a temporality of signification), perfectly described by Eisenstein himself when he jubilantly quotes the golden rule of the old K. S. Gillette: *'just short of the cutting edge'*.

The obtuse meaning, then, has something to do with disguise. Look at Ivan's beard raised to obtuse meaning, in my opinion, in image VII; it declares its artifice but without in so doing abandoning the 'good faith' of its referent (the historical figure of the czar): an actor disguised twice over (once as actor in the anecdote, once as actor in the dramaturgy) without one disguise destroying the other; a multi-layering of meanings which always lets the previous meaning continue, as in a geological formation, saying the opposite without giving up the contrary – a (two-term) dramatic dialectic that Brecht would have liked. The Eisensteinian 'artifice' is at once falsification of itself – pastiche – and derisory fetish, since it shows its fissure and its suture: what can be seen in image VII is the join and thus the initial disjoin of the beard perpendicular to the chin. That the top of a head (the most 'obtuse' part of the human person), that a single bun of hair (in image VIII) can be the *expression* of grief, that is what is derisory – for the expression, not for the grief. Hence no parody, no trace of burlesque; there is no aping of grief (the obvious meaning must remain revolutionary, the general mourning which accompanies Vakulinchuk's death has a historical meaning), and yet, 'embodied' in the bun, it has a cut-off, a refusal of contamination; the populism of the woollen shawl (obvious meaning) stops at the bun; here begins the fetish – the hair – and a kind of *non-negating derision* of the expression. The whole of the obtuse meaning (its disruptive force) is staked on the excessive mass of the hair. Look at another bun (that of the woman in image IX): it contradicts the tiny raised fist, atrophies it without the reduction having the slightest symbolic (intellectual) value; prolonged by small curls, pulling the face in towards an ovine model, it gives the woman something *touching* (in the way that a certain generous foolishness can be) or *sensitive* – these antiquated words, mystified words if ever there were, with little that is revolutionary or political about them, must nevertheless be assumed. I believe that the obtuse meaning carries a certain *emotion*. Caught up in the disguise, such emotion is never sticky, it is an emotion which simply *designates* what one loves, what one wants to defend: an emotion-value, an evaluation. Everyone will agree, I think, that SME's proletarian ethnography fragmented the length of Vakulinchuk's funeral, is constantly informed by something loving (using the word regardless of any specification as to age or sex). Maternal, cordial, virile, 'sympathetic' without any recourse to stereotypes, the Eisensteinian people is essentially *lovable*. We savour, we love the two round-capped heads in image X, we enter into complicity, into an understanding with them. Doubtless beauty can work as an obtuse meaning; this is the case in image XI, where the extremely dense obvious meaning (Ivan's attitude, young Vladimir's half-wit foolishness) is anchored and/or set adrift by Basmanov's beauty. But the eroticism included in the obtuse meaning (or rather: the eroticism which this meaning picks up) is no respector of the aesthetic: Euphrosyne is ugly, 'obtuse' (images XII and XIII), like the monk (image XIV), but this obtuseness exceeds the anecdote, becomes a blunting of meaning, its drifting. There is in the obtuse meaning an eroticism which includes the contrary of the beautiful, as also what falls outside such contrariety, its limit – inversion, unease, and perhaps sadism. Look at the flabby innocence of the 'Children in the Fiery Furnace' (image XV), the schoolboyish ridicule of their mufflers dutifully tucked up to the chin, the curds-and-whey skin (of their eyes, of their mouths set in the skin) which Fellini seems to have remembered in the hermaphrodite of his *Satiricon* – the very same mentioned by Georges Bataille, notably in that text in *Documents* which situates for me one of the possible regions of obtuse meaning, 'The big toe'.[1]

Let us continue (if these examples will suffice to lead on to one or two more theoretical remarks). The obtuse meaning is not in the language-system (even that of symbols). Take away the obtuse meaning and communication and signification still remain, still circulate, still come through: without it, I can still state and read. No more, however, is it to be located in language use. It may be that there is a certain constant in Eisensteinian obtuse meaning, but in that case it is already a thematic language, an idiolect, this idiolect being provisional (simply decided by a critic writing a book on SME). Obtuse meanings are to be found not everywhere (the signifier is rare, a future figure) but *somewhere*: in other *authors* of films (perhaps), in a certain manner of reading 'life' and so 'reality' itself (the word is simply used here in opposition to the deliberately fictive). In image XVI from *Ordinary Fascism* (by Mikhail Romm), a documentary image, I can easily read an obvious meaning, that of fascism (aesthetics and symbolics of power, the theatrical hunt), but I can also read an obtuse meaning: the (again) disguised, blond silliness of the young quiver-bearer, the flabbiness of his hands and mouth (I cannot manage to describe, only to designate a location), Goering's thick nails, his trashy ring (this already on the brink of obvious meaning, like the treacly platitude of the imbecile smile of the bespectacled man in the background – visibly an 'arse-licker'). In other words, the obtuse meaning is not situated structurally, a semantologist would not agree as to its objective existence (but then what is an objective reading?); and if to me it is clear (to me), that is *still* perhaps (for the moment) by the same 'aberration' which compelled the lone and unhappy Saussure to hear in ancient poetry the

1. [Georges Bataille, 'Le gros orteil', *Documents*, Paris 1968, pp. 75–82.]

enigmatic voice of anagram, unoriginated and obsessive. Same uncertainty when it is a matter of *describing* the obtuse meaning (of giving an idea of where it is going, where it goes away). The obtuse meaning is a signifier without a signified, hence the difficulty in naming it. My reading remains suspended between the image and its description, between definition and approximation. If the obtuse meaning cannot be described, that is because, in contrast to the obvious meaning, it does not copy anything – how do you describe something that does not represent anything? The pictorial 'rendering' of words is here impossible, with the consequence that if, in front of these images, we remain, you and I, at the level of articulated language – at the level, that is, of my own text – the obtuse meaning will not succeed in existing, in entering the critic's metalanguage. Which means that the obtuse meaning is outside (articulated) language while nevertheless within interlocution. For if you look at the images I am discussing, you can see this meaning, we can agree on it 'over the shoulder' or 'on the back' of articulated language. Thanks to the image (fixed, it is true; a factor which will be taken up later) or much rather thanks to what, in the image, is purely image (which is in fact very little), we do without language yet never cease to understand one another.

In short, what the obtuse meaning disturbs, sterilizes, is metalanguage (criticism). A number of reasons can be given for this. First and foremost, obtuse meaning is discontinuous, indifferent to the story and to the obvious meaning (as signification of the story). This dissociation has a de-naturing or at least a distancing effect with regard to the referent (to 'reality' as nature, the realist instance). Eisenstein would probably have acknowledged this incongruity, this im-pertinence of the signifier, Eisenstein who tells us concerning sound and colour: 'Art begins the moment the creaking of a boot on the sound-track

occurs against a different visual shot and thus gives rise
to corresponding associations. It is the same with colour:
colour begins where it no longer corresponds to natural
colouration . . .' Then, the signifier (the third meaning) is
not filled out, it keeps a permanent state of *depletion* (a
word from linguistics which designates empty, all-purpose
verbs, as for example the French verb *faire*). We could also
say on the contrary – and it would be just as correct – that
this same signifier is not empty (cannot empty itself), that it
maintains a state of perpetual erethism, desire not finding
issue in that spasm of the signified which normally brings
the subject voluptuously back into the peace of nomin-
ations. Finally, the obtuse meaning can be seen as an
accent, the very form of an emergence, of a fold (a crease
even) marking the heavy layer of informations and significations. If it could be described (a contradiction in terms),
it would have exactly the nature of the Japanese *haiku* –
anaphoric gesture without significant content, a sort of
gash rased of meaning (of desire for meaning). Thus in
image V:

> Mouth drawn, eyes shut squinting,
> Headscarf low over forehead,
> She weeps.

This accent – the simultaneously emphatic and elliptic
character of which has already been mentioned – is not
directed towards meaning (as in hysteria), does not theatrica-
lize (Eisensteinian decorativism belongs to another level),
does not even indicate an *elsewhere* of meaning (another
content, added to the obvious meaning); it outplays meaning
– subverts not the content but the whole practice of meaning. A new – rare – practice affirmed against a majority
practice (that of signification), obtuse meaning appears
necessarily as a luxury, an expenditure with no exchange.
This luxury does not *yet* belong to today's politics but

nevertheless *already* to tomorrow's.

Something has still to be said concerning the syntagmatic responsibility of the third meaning: what is its place in the movement of the anecdote, in the logico-temporal system without which, so it seems, it is impossible to communicate a narrative to the 'mass' of readers and spectators? It is clear that the obtuse meaning is the epitome of a counter-narrative; disseminated, reversible, set to its own temporality, it inevitably determines (if one follows it) a quite different analytical segmentation to that in shots, sequences and syntagms (technical or narrative) – an extraordinary segmentation: counter-logical and yet 'true'. Imagine 'following' not Euphrosyne's schemings, nor even the character (as diegetic entity or symbolic figure), nor even, again, the face of the Wicked Mother, but merely, in this face, this attitude, this black veil, the heavy, ugly flatness– you will then have a different time-scale, neither diegetic nor oneiric, a different film. A theme with neither variations nor development (the obvious meaning is fully thematic: there is a theme of the Funeral), the obtuse meaning can only come and go, appearing-disappearing. The play of presence/absence undermines the character, making of it a simple nub of facets; a disjunction expressed in another connection by SME himself: '*What is characteristic is that the different positions of one and the same czar . . . are given without link between one position and the next.*'

Precisely. The *indifference* or freedom of position of the supplementary signifier in relation to the narrative allows us to situate with some exactitude the historical, political, theoretical task accomplished by Eisenstein. In his work, the story (the diegetic, anecdotal representation) is not destroyed – quite the contrary: what finer story than that of *Ivan* or *Potemkin*? This importance given to the narrative is necessary in order *to be understood* in a society which, unable to resolve the contradictions of history without a long political transaction, draws support (provisionally?) from mythical (narrative) solutions. The *contemporary* problem is not to destroy the narrative but to subvert it; today's task is to dissociate subversion from destruction. It seems to me that SME operates such a distinction: the presence of an obtuse, supplementary, third meaning – if only in a few images, but then as an imperishable signature, as a seal endorsing the whole of the work (and the whole of his work) – radically recasts the theoretical status of the anecdote: the story (the diegesis) is no longer just a strong system (the millennial system of narrative) but also and contradictorily a simple space, a field of permanences and permutations. It becomes that configuration, that stage, whose false limits multiply the signifier's permutational play, that vast trace which, by difference, compels what SME himself calls a *vertical* reading, that *false* order which permits the turning of the pure series, the aleatory combination (chance is crude, a signifier on the cheap) and the attainment of a structuration *which slips away from the inside*. It can thus be said that with SME we have to reverse the cliché according to which the more gratuitous a meaning, the more it will appear as a mere parasite of the story being narrated; on the contrary, it is this story which here finds itself in some sort parametric to the signifier for which it is now merely the field of displacement, the constitutive negativity, or, again, the fellow-traveller.

In other words, the third meaning structures the film *differently* without – at least in SME – subverting the story and for this reason, perhaps, it is at the level of the third meaning, and at that level alone, that the 'filmic' finally emerges. The filmic is that in the film which cannot be described, the representation which cannot be represented. The filmic begins only where language and metalanguage end. Everything that can be *said* about *Ivan* or *Potemkin* can be said of a written text (entitled *Ivan the Terrible* or

Battleship Potemkin) except this, the obtuse meaning; I can gloss everything in Euphrosyne, except the obtuse quality of her face. The filmic, then, lies precisely here, in that region where articulated language is no longer more than approximative and where another language begins (whose science, therefore, cannot be linguistics, soon discarded like a booster rocket). The third meaning – theoretically locatable but not describable – can now be seen as the *passage* from language to *signifiance* and the founding act of the filmic itself. Forced to develop in a civilization of the signified, it is not surprising that (despite the incalculable number of films in the world) the filmic should still be rare (a few flashes in SME, perhaps elsewhere?), so much so that it could be said that as yet the film does not exist (any more than does the text); there is only 'cinema', language, narrative, poetry, sometimes extremely 'modern', 'translated' into 'images' said to be 'animated'. Nor is it surprising that the filmic can only be located after having – analytically – gone across the 'essential', the 'depth' and the 'complexity' of the cinematic work; all those riches which are merely those of articulated language, with which we constitute the work and believe we exhaust it. The filmic is not the same as the film, is as far removed from the film as the novelistic is from the novel (I can write in the novelistic without ever writing novels).

The still

Which is why to a certain extent (the extent of our theoretical fumblings) the filmic, very paradoxically, cannot be grasped in the film 'in situation', 'in movement', 'in its natural state', but only in that major artefact, the still. For a long time, I have been intrigued by the phenomenon of being interested and even fascinated by photos from a film (outside a cinema, in the pages of *Cahiers du cinéma*) and

of then losing everything of those photos (not just the capti-
vation but the memory of the image) when once inside the
viewing room – a change which can even result in a complete reversal of values. I at first ascribed this taste for stills
to my lack of cinematic culture, to my resistance to film;
I thought of myself as like those children who prefer the
pictures to the text, or like those clients who, unable to
attain the adult possession of objects (because too expensive),
are content to derive pleasure from looking at a choice of
samples or a department store catalogue. Such an explanation does no more than reproduce the common opinion
with regard to stills which sees them as a remote sub-
product of the film, a sample, a means of drawing in custom,
a pornographic extract, and, technically, a reduction of
the work by the immobilization of what is taken to be the
sacred essence of cinema – the movement of the images.

If, however, the specific filmic (the filmic of the future)
lies not in movement, but in an inarticulable third meaning
that neither the simple photograph nor figurative painting
can assume since they lack the diegetic horizon, the possibility of configuration mentioned earlier,[1] then the 'movement' regarded as the essence of film is not animation, flux,

1. There are other 'arts' which combine still (or at least drawing)
and story, diegesis – namely the photo-novel and the comic-strip. I am
convinced that these 'arts', born in the lower depths of high culture,
possess theoretical qualifications and present a new signifier (related
to the obtuse meaning). This is acknowledged as regards the comic-
strip but I myself experience this slight trauma of *significance* faced with
certain photo-novels: '*their stupidity touches me*' (which could be
a certain definition of obtuse meaning). There may thus be a future –
or a very ancient past – truth in these derisory, vulgar, foolish, dialogical
forms of consumer subculture. And there is an autonomous 'art' (a
'text'), that of the *pictogram* ('anecdotalized' images, obtuse meanings
placed in a diegetic space); this art taking across historically and cultur-
ally heteroclite productions: ethnographic pictograms, stained glass
windows, Carpaccio's *Legend of Saint Ursula*, *images d'Epinal*, photo-
novels, comic-strips. The innovation represented by the still (in comparison with these other pictograms) would be that the filmic (which
it constitutes) is *doubled* by another text, the film.

mobility, 'life', copy, but simply the framework of a permutational unfolding and a theory of the still becomes necessary, a theory whose possible points of departure must be given briefly here in conclusion.

The still offers us the *inside* of the fragment. In this connection we would need to take up – displacing them – Eisenstein's own formulations when envisaging the new possibilities of audio-visual montage: '. . . the basic centre of gravity . . . is transferred to *inside* the fragment, into the elements included in the image itself. *And the centre of gravity is no longer the element "between shots" – the shock – but the element "inside the shot" – the accentuation within the fragment* . . .' Of course, there is no audio-visual montage in the still, but SME's formula is general insofar as it establishes a right to the syntagmatic disjunction of images and calls for a *vertical* reading of the articulation. Moreover, the still is not a sample (an idea that supposes a sort of homogeneous, statistical nature of the film elements) but a quotation (we know how much importance presently accrues to this concept in the theory of the text): at once parodic and disseminatory. It is not a specimen chemically extracted from the substance of the film, but rather the trace of a superior *distribution* of traits of which the film as experienced in its animated flow would give no more than one text among others. The still, then, is the fragment of a second text *whose existence never exceeds the fragment*; film and still find themselves in a palimpsest relationship without it being possible to say that one is *on top of* the other or that one is *extracted* from the other. Finally, the still throws off the constraint of filmic time; which constraint is extremely powerful, continuing to form an obstacle to what might be called the adult birth of film (born technically, occasionally even aesthetically, film has still to be born theoretically). For written texts, unless they are very conventional, totally committed to logico-temporal order, reading time is free; for film, this is not so, since the image cannot go faster or slower without losing its perceptual figure. The still, by instituting a reading that is at once instantaneous and vertical, scorns logical time (which is only an operational time); it teaches us how to dissociate the technical constraint from what is the specific filmic and which is the 'indescribable' meaning. Perhaps it was the reading of *this other text* (here in stills) that SME called for when he said that a film is not simply to be seen and heard but to be scrutinized and listened to attentively. This seeing and this hearing are obviously not the postulation of some simple need to apply the mind (that would be banal, a pious wish) but rather a veritable mutation of reading and its object, text or film – which is a crucial problem of our time.

Diderot, Brecht, Eisenstein

For André Techiné

Let us imagine that an affinity of status and history has linked mathematics and acoustics since the ancient Greeks. Let us also imagine that for two or three millennia this effectively Pythagorean space has been somewhat repressed (Pythagoras is indeed the eponymous hero of Secrecy). Finally, let us imagine that from the time of these same Greeks another relationship has been established over against the first and has got the better of it, continually taking the lead in the history of the arts – the relationship between geometry and theatre. The theatre is precisely that practice which calculates the place of things *as they are observed*: if I set the spectacle here, the spectator will see this; if I put it elsewhere, he will not, and I can avail myself of this masking effect and play on the illusion it provides. The stage is the line which stands across the path of the optic pencil, tracing at once the point at which it is brought to a stop and, as it were, the threshold of its ramification. Thus is founded – against music (against the text) – *representation*.

Representation is not defined directly by imitation: even if one gets rid of notions of the 'real', of the 'vraisemblable', of the 'copy', there will still be representation for so long as a subject (author, reader, spectator or voyeur) casts his *gaze* towards a horizon on which he cuts out the base of a triangle, his eye (or his mind) forming the apex. The 'Organon of Representation' (which it is today becoming possible to write because there are intimations of *something else*) will have as its dual foundation the sovereignty of the act of cutting out [*découpage*] and the unity of the subject of that action. The substance of the various arts will therefore be of little importance; certainly, theatre and cinema are direct expressions of geometry (unless, as rarely, they carry out some research on the voice, on stereophony), but classic (readable) literary discourse, which has for such a long time now abandoned prosody, music, is also a representational, geometrical discourse in that it cuts out segments in order to depict them: to discourse (the classics would have said) is simply 'to depict the tableau one has in one's mind'. The scene, the picture, the shot, the cut-out rectangle, here we have the very *condition* that allows us to conceive theatre, painting, cinema, literature, all those arts, that is, other than music and which could be called *dioptric arts*. (Counter-proof: nothing permits us to locate the slightest tableau in the musical text, except by reducing it to a subservience to drama; nothing permits us to cut out in it the slightest fetish, except by debasing it through the use of trite melodies.)

As is well known, the whole of Diderot's aesthetics rests on the identification of theatrical scene and pictorial tableau: the perfect play is a succession of tableaux, that is, a gallery, an exhibition; the stage offers the spectator 'as many real tableaux as there are in the action moments favourable to the painter'. The tableau (pictorial, theatrical, literary) is a pure cut-out segment with clearly defined edges, irreversible and incorruptible; everything that surrounds it is banished into nothingness, remains unnamed, while everything that it admits within its field is promoted into essence, into light, into view. Such demiurgic discrimination implies high quality of thought: the tableau is intellectual, it has something to say (something moral, social) but it also says that it knows how this must be done; it is simultaneously significant and propaedeutical, impressive and reflexive, moving and conscious of the channels of emotion. The epic scene in Brecht, the shot in Eisenstein are so many tableaux; they are scenes which are *laid out* (in the sense in which one says *the table is laid*), which answer perfectly to that dramatic unity theorized by Diderot: firmly cut out (remember the tolerance shown by Brecht with regard to the Italian curtain-stage, his contempt for indefinite theatres – open air, theatre in the round), erecting a meaning but manifesting the production of that meaning, they accomplish the coincidence of the visual and the ideal *découpages*. Nothing separates the shot in Eisenstein from the picture by Greuze (except, of course, their respective projects: in the latter moral, in the former social); nothing separates the scene in epic theatre from the Eisenstein shot (except that in Brecht the tableau is offered to the spectator for criticism, not for adherence).

Is the tableau then (since it arises from a process of cutting out) a fetish-object? Yes, at the level of the ideal meaning (Good, Progress, the Cause, the triumph of the just History); no, at that of its composition. Or rather, more exactly, it is the very *composition* that allows the displacement of the point at which the fetish comes to a halt and thus the setting further back of the loving effect of the *découpage*. Once again, Diderot is for us the theorist of this dialectic of desire; in the article on 'Composition', he writes: 'A well-composed picture [*tableau*] is a whole contained under a single point of view, in which the parts work together to one end and form by their mutual correspondence a unity as real as that of the members of the body of an animal; so that a piece of painting made up of a large number of figures thrown at random on to the canvas, with neither proportion, intelligence nor unity, no more deserves to be called a *true composition* than scattered studies of legs, nose and eyes on the same cartoon deserve to be called a *portrait* or even a *human figure*.' Thus is the body expressly introduced into the idea of the tableau, but it is the whole body that is so introduced – the organs, grouped together and as though held in cohesion by the magnetic power of the segmentation, function in the name of a transcendence, that of the *figure*, which receives the full fetishistic load and becomes the sublime substitute of meaning: it is this meaning that is fetishized. (Doubtless there would be no difficulty in finding in post-Brechtian theatre and post-Eisensteinian cinema *mises en scène* marked by the dispersion of the tableau, the pulling to pieces of the 'composition', the setting in movement of the 'partial organs' of the human figure, in short the holding in check of the metaphysical meaning of the work – but then also of its political meaning; or, at least, the carrying over of this meaning towards *another* politics).

Brecht indicated clearly that in epic theatre (which proceeds by successive tableaux) all the burden of meaning and pleasure bears on each scene, not on the whole. At the level of the play itself, there is no development, no maturation; there is indeed an ideal meaning (given straight in every tableau), but there is no final meaning, nothing but a series of segmentations each of which possesses a sufficient demonstrative power. The same is true in Eisenstein: the film is a contiguity of episodes, each one absolutely meaningful, aesthetically perfect, and the result is a cinema by vocation anthological, itself holding out to the fetishist, with dotted lines, the piece for him to cut out and take away to enjoy (isn't it said that in some *cinémathèque* or other a piece of film is missing from the copy of *Battleship Potemkin* – the scene with the baby's pram, of course – it having been cut off and stolen lovingly like a lock of hair, a glove or an item of women's underwear?). The primary force of Eisenstein is due to the fact that *no image is boring*, you are not obliged to wait for the next in order to understand and be delighted; it is a question not of a dialectic (that time of the patience required for certain pleasures) but of a continuous jubilation made up of a summation of perfect instants.

Naturally, Diderot had conceived of this perfect instant (and had given it thought). In order to tell a story, the painter has only an instant at his disposal, the instant he is going to immobilize on the canvas, and he must thus choose it well, assuring it in advance of the greatest possible yield of meaning and pleasure. Necessarily total, this instant will be artificial (unreal; this is not a realist art), a hieroglyph in which can be read at a single glance (at one grasp, if we think in terms of theatre and cinema) the present, the past and the future; that is, the historical meaning of the represented action. This crucial instant, totally concrete and totally abstract, is what Lessing subsequently calls (in the *Laocoon*) the *pregnant moment*. Brecht's theatre, Eisenstein's cinema are series of pregnant moments: when Mother Courage bites on the coin offered by the recruiting sergeant and, as a result of this brief interval of distrust, loses her son, she demonstrates at once her past as tradeswoman and the future that awaits her – all her children dead in consequence of her money-making blindness. When (in *The General Line*) the peasant woman lets her skirt be ripped up for material to help in repairing the tractor, the gesture bears the weight of a history: its pregnancy brings together the past victory (the tractor bitterly won from bureaucratic incompetence), the present struggle and the effectiveness of solidarity. The pregnant moment is just this presence of all the absences (memories, lessons, promises) to whose rhythm History becomes both intelligible and desirable.

In Brecht, it is the *social gest* which takes up the idea of the pregnant moment. What then is a social gest (how much irony has reactionary criticism poured on this Brechtian concept, one of the clearest and most intelligent that dramatic theory has ever produced!)? It is a gesture or set of gestures (but never a gesticulation) in which a whole social situation can be read. Not every gest is social: there is nothing social in the movements a man makes in order to brush off a fly; but if this same man, poorly dressed, is struggling against guard-dogs, the gest becomes social. The action by which the canteen-woman tests the genuineness of the money offered is a social gest; as again is the excessive flourish with which the bureaucrat of *The General Line* signs his official papers. This kind of social gest can be traced even in language itself. A language can be gestual, says Brecht, when it indicates certain attitudes that the speaker adopts towards others: 'If thine eye offend thee, pluck it out' is more gestual than 'Pluck out the eye that offends thee' because the order of the sentence and the asyndeton that carries it along refer to a prophetic and vengeful situation. Thus rhetorical forms may be gestual, which is why it is pointless to criticize Eisenstein's art (as also that of Brecht) for being 'formalizing' or 'aesthetic': form, aesthetic, rhetoric can be socially responsible if they are handled with deliberation. Representation (since that is what we are concerned with) has inescapably to reckon with the social gest; as soon as one 'represents' (cuts out, marks off the tableau and so discontinues the overall totality), it must be decided whether the gesture is social or not (when it refers not to a particular society but to Man).

What does the actor do in the tableau (the scene, the shot)? Since the tableau is the presentation of an ideal meaning, the actor must present the very knowledge of the meaning, for the latter would not be ideal if it did not bring with it its own machination. This knowledge which the actor must demonstrate – by an unwonted supplement – is, however, neither his human knowledge (his tears must not refer simply to the state of feeling of the Downcast) nor his knowledge as actor (he must not show that he knows how to act well). The actor must prove that he is not enslaved to the spectator (bogged down in 'reality', in 'humanity'), that he guides meaning towards its ideality – a sovereignty of the actor, master of meaning, which is evident in Brecht, since he theorized it under the term 'distanciation'. It is no less evident in Eisenstein (at least in the author of *The General Line* which is my example here), and this not as a result of a ceremonial, ritual art – the kind of art called for by Brecht – but through the insistence of the social gest which never ceases to stamp the actors' gestures (fists clenching, hands gripping tools, peasants reporting at the bureaucrat's reception-desk). Nevertheless, it is true that in Eisenstein, as in Greuze (for Diderot an exemplary painter), the actor does sometimes adopt expressions of the most pathetic quality, a pathos which can appear to be very little 'distanced'; but distanciation is a properly Brechtian method, vital to Brecht because he represents a tableau for the spectator to criticize; in the other two, the actor does not necessarily have to distance: what he has to present is an ideal meaning and it is sufficient therefore that he 'bring out' the production of this value, that he render it tangible, intellectually visible, by the very excess of the versions he gives it; his expression then signifies an idea – which is why it is excessive – not some natural quality. All this is a far cry from the facial affectations of the Actors' Studio, the much praised 'restraint' of which has no other meaning than its contribution to the personal glory of the actor (witness in this respect Brando's grimacings in *The Last Tango in Paris*).

Does the tableau have a subject (a topic)? Nowise; it has a meaning, not a subject. The meaning begins with the social gest (with the pregnant moment); outside of the gest, there is only vagueness, insignificance. 'In a way,' writes Brecht, 'subjects always have a certain naivety, they are somewhat lacking in qualities. Empty, they are in some sort sufficient to themselves. Only the social *gest* (criticism, strategy, irony, propaganda, etc.) introduces the human element.' To which Diderot adds (if one may put it like that): the creation of the painter or the dramatist lies not in the choice of a subject but in the choice of the pregnant moment, in the choice of the tableau. It matters little, after all, that Eisenstein took his 'subjects' from the past history of Russia and the Revolution and not – 'as he should have done' (so say his censors today) – from the present of the construction of socialism (except in the case of *The General Line*); battleship or czar are of minor importance, are merely vague and empty 'subjects', what alone counts is the gest, the critical demonstration of the gesture, its inscription – to whatever period it may belong – in a text the social machination of which is clearly visible: the subject neither adds nor subtracts anything. How many films are there now 'about' drugs, in which drugs is the 'subject'? But this is a subject that is hollow; without any social gest, drugs are insignificant, or rather, their significance is simply that of an essential nature – vague, empty, eternal: 'drugs lead to impotence' (*Trash*), 'drugs lead to suicide' (*Absences répétées*). The subject is a false articulation: why this subject in preference to another? The work only begins with the tableau, when the meaning is set into the gesture and the co-ordination of gestures. Take *Mother Courage*: you may be certain of a misunderstanding if you think that its 'subject' is the Thirty Years War, or even the denunciation of war in general; its *gest* is not there, but in the blindness of the tradeswoman who believes herself to live off war only, in fact, to die of it; even more, the gest lies in the *view* that I, spectator, have of this blindness.

In the theatre, in the cinema, in traditional literature, things are always seen *from somewhere*. Here we have the geometrical foundation of representation: a fetishist subject is required to cut out the tableau. This point of meaning is always the Law: law of society, law of struggle, law of meaning. Thus all militant art cannot but be representational, legal. In order for representation to be really bereft of origin and exceed its geometrical nature without ceasing to be representation, the price that must be paid is enormous – no less than death. In Dreyer's *Vampyr*, as a friend points out, the camera moves from house to cemetery recording *what the dead man sees*: such is the extreme limit at which representation is outplayed; the spectator can no longer take up any position, for he cannot identify his eye with the closed eyes of the dead man; the tableau has no point of departure, no support, it gapes open. Everything that goes on before this limit is reached (and this is the case of the work of Brecht and Eisenstein) can only be legal: in the long run, it is the Law of the Party which cuts out the epic scene, the filmic shot; it is this Law which looks, frames, focusses, enunciates. Once again Eisenstein and Brecht rejoin Diderot (promoter of bourgeois domestic tragedy, as his two successors were the promoters of a socialist art). Diderot distinguished in painting major practices, those whose force is cathartic, aiming at the ideality of meaning, from minor practices, those which are purely imitative, anecdotal – the difference between Greuze and Chardin. In other words, in a period of ascendency every physics of art (Chardin) must be crowned with a meta-physics (Greuze). In Brecht, in Eisenstein, Chardin and Greuze co-exist (more complex, Brecht leaves it to his public to be the Greuze of the Chardin he sets before their eyes). How could art, in a society that has not yet found peace, cease to be metaphysical? that is, significant, read-able, representational? fetishist? When are we to have music, the Text?

It seems that Brecht knew hardly anything of Diderot (barely, perhaps, the *Paradoxe sur le comédien*). He it is, however, who authorizes, in a quite contingent way, the tripartite conjuncture that has just been proposed. Round about 1937, Brecht had the idea of founding a *Diderot Society*, a place for pooling theatrical experiments and studies – doubtless because he saw in Diderot, in addition to the figure of a great materialist philosopher, a man of the theatre whose theory aimed at dispensing equally pleasure and instruction. Brecht drew up the programme for this Society and produced a tract which he contemplated sending out. To whom? To Piscator, to Jean Renoir, to Eisenstein.

Introduction to the Structural Analysis of Narratives

The narratives of the world are numberless. Narrative is first and foremost a prodigious variety of genres, themselves distributed amongst different substances – as though any material were fit to receive man's stories. Able to be carried by articulated language, spoken or written, fixed or moving images, gestures, and the ordered mixture of all these substances; narrative is present in myth, legend, fable, tale, novella, epic, history, tragedy, drama, comedy, mime, painting (think of Carpaccio's *Saint Ursula*), stained glass windows, cinema, comics, news item, conversation. Moreover, under this almost infinite diversity of forms, narrative is present in every age, in every place, in every society; it begins with the very history of mankind and there nowhere is nor has been a people without narrative. All classes, all human groups, have their narratives, enjoyment of which is very often shared by men with different, even opposing,[1] cultural backgrounds. Caring nothing for the division between good and bad literature, narrative is international. transhistorical, transcultural: it is simply there, like life itself.

Must we conclude from this universality that narrative is insignificant? Is it so general that we can have nothing to say about it except for the modest description of a few highly individualized varieties, something literary history occasionally undertakes? But then how are we to master even these varieties, how are we to justify our right to

1. It must be remembered that this is not the case with either poetry or the essay, both of which are dependent on the cultural level of their consumers.

differentiate and identify them? How is novel to be set against novella, tale against myth, drama against tragedy (as has been done a thousand times) without reference to a common model? Such a model is implied by every proposition relating to the most individual, the most historical, of narrative forms. It is thus legitimate that, far from the abandoning of any idea of dealing with narrative on the grounds of its universality, there should have been (from Aristotle on) a periodic interest in narrative form and it is normal that the newly developing structuralism should make this form one of its first concerns – is not structuralism's constant aim to master the infinity of utterances [*paroles*] by describing the 'language' ['*langue*'] of which they are the products and from which they can be generated. Faced with the infinity of narratives, the multiplicity of standpoints – historical, psychological, sociological, ethnological, aesthetic, etc. – from which they can be studied, the analyst finds himself in more or less the same situation as Saussure confronted by the heterogeneity of language [*langage*] and seeking to extract a principle of classification and a central focus for description from the apparent confusion of the individual messages. Keeping simply to modern times, the Russian Formalists, Propp and Lévi-Strauss have taught us to recognize the following dilemma: either a narrative is merely a rambling collection of events, in which case nothing can be said about it other than by referring back to the storyteller's (the author's) art, talent or genius – all mythical forms of chance[1] – or else it shares with other narratives a common structure which is open to analysis, no matter how much patience its formulation requires. There is a world of difference between the most complex randomness

1. There does, of course, exist an 'art' of the storyteller, which is the ability to generate narratives (messages) from the structure (the code). This art corresponds to the notion of *performance* in Chomsky and is far removed from the 'genius' of the author, romantically conceived as some barely explicable personal secret.

and the most elementary combinatory scheme, and it is impossible to combine (to produce) a narrative without reference to an implicit system of units and rules.

Where then are we to look for the structures of narrative? Doubtless, in narratives themselves. *Each and every* narrative? Many commentators who accept the idea of a narrative structure are nevertheless unable to resign themselves to dissociating literary analysis from the example of the experimental sciences; nothing daunted, they ask that a purely inductive method be applied to narrative and that one start by studying all the narratives within a genre, a period, a society. This commonsense view is utopian. Linguistics itself, with only some three thousand languages to embrace, cannot manage such a programme and has wisely turned deductive, a step which in fact marked its veritable constitution as a science and the beginning of its spectacular progress, it even succeeding in anticipating facts prior to their discovery.[1] So what of narrative analysis, faced as it is with millions of narratives? Of necessity, it is condemned to a deductive procedure, obliged first to devise a hypothetical model of description (what American linguists call a 'theory') and then gradually to work down from this model towards the different narrative species which at once conform to and depart from the model. It is only at the level of these conformities and departures that analysis will be able to come back to, but now equipped with a single descriptive tool, the plurality of narratives, to their historical, geographical and cultural diversity.[2]

1. See the history of the Hittite *a*, postulated by Saussure and actually discovered fifty years later, as given in Emile Benveniste, *Problèmes de linguistique générale*, Paris 1966, p. 35 [*Problems of General Linguistics*, Coral Gables, Florida 1971, p. 32].

2. Let us bear in mind the present conditions of linguistic description: '. . . linguistic "structure" is always relative not just to the data or corpus but also to the grammatical theory describing the data' E. Bach, *An Introduction to Transformational Grammars*, New York 1964, p. 29; 'it has been recognized that language must be described as a

Thus, in order to describe and classify the infinite number of narratives, a 'theory' (in this pragmatic sense) is needed and the immediate task is that of finding it, of starting to define it. Its development can be greatly facilitated if one begins from a model able to provide it with its initial terms and principles. In the current state of research, it seems reasonable[1] that the structural analysis of narrative be given linguistics itself as founding model.

I. The Language of Narrative

1. Beyond the sentence

As we know, linguistics stops at the sentence, the last unit which it considers to fall within its scope. If the sentence, being an order and not a series, cannot be reduced to the sum of the words which compose it and constitutes thereby a specific unit, a piece of discourse, on the contrary, is no more than the succession of the sentences composing it. From the point of view of linguistics, there is nothing in discourse that is not to be found in the sentence: 'The sentence,' writes Martinet, 'is the smallest segment that is perfectly and wholly representative of discourse.'[2] Hence there can be no question of linguistics setting itself an object superior to the sentence, since beyond the sentence

formal structure, but that the description first of all necessitates specification of adequate procedures and criteria and that, finally, the reality of the object is inseparable from the method given for its description', Benveniste, op. cit., p. 119 [trans. p. 101].

1. But not imperative: see Claude Bremond, 'La logique des possibles narratifs', *Communications* 8, 1966, which is more logical than linguistic. [Bremond's various studies in this field have now been collected in a volume entitled, precisely, *Logique du récit*, Paris 1973; his work consists in the analysis of narrative according to the pattern of possible alternatives, each narrative moment – or function – giving rise to a set of different possible resolutions, the actualization of any one of which in turn produces a new set of alternatives.]

2. André Martinet, 'Réflexions sur la phrase', in *Language and Society* (Studies presented to Jansen), Copenhagen 1961, p. 113.

are only more sentences – having described the flower, the botanist is not to get involved in describing the bouquet.

And yet it is evident that discourse itself (as a set of sentences) is organized and that, through this organization, it can be seen as the message of another language, one operating at a higher level than the language of the linguists.[1] Discourse has its units, its rules, its 'grammar': beyond the sentence, and though consisting solely of sentences, it must naturally form the object of a second linguistics. For a long time indeed, such a linguistics of discourse bore a glorious name, that of Rhetoric. As a result of a complex historical movement, however, in which Rhetoric went over to belles-lettres and the latter was divorced from the study of language, it has recently become necessary to take up the problem afresh. The new linguistics of discourse has still to be developed, but at least it is being postulated, and by the linguists themselves.[2] This last fact is not without significance, for, although constituting an autonomous object, discourse must be studied from the basis of linguistics. If a working hypothesis is needed for an analysis whose task is immense and whose materials infinite, then the most reasonable thing is to posit a homological relation between sentence and discourse insofar as it is likely that a similar formal organization orders all semiotic systems, whatever their substances and dimensions. A discourse is a long 'sentence' (the units of which are not necessarily sentences), just as a sentence, allowing for certain specifications, is a short 'discourse'. This hypothesis accords well with a number of propositions put forward in contemporary anthro-

1. It goes without saying, as Jakobson has noted, that between the sentence and what lies beyond the sentence there are transitions; co-ordination, for instance, can work over the limit of the sentence.

2. See especially: Benveniste, op. cit., Chapter 10; Z. S. Harris, 'Discourse Analysis', *Language* 28, 1952, pp. 18–23 & 474–94; N. Ruwet, 'Analyse structurale d'un poème français', *Linguistics* 3, 1964, pp. 62–83.

pology. Jakobson and Lévi-Strauss have pointed out that mankind can be defined by the ability to create secondary – 'self-multiplying' – systems (tools for the manufacture of other tools, double articulation of language, incest taboo permitting the fanning out of families) while the Soviet linguist Ivanov supposes that artificial languages can only have been acquired after natural language: what is important for men is to have the use of several systems of meaning and natural language helps in the elaboration of artificial languages. It is therefore legitimate to posit a 'secondary' relation between sentence and discourse – a relation which will be referred to as homological, in order to respect the purely formal nature of the correspondences.

The general language [*langue*] of narrative is one (and clearly only one) of the idioms apt for consideration by the linguistics of discourse[1] and it accordingly comes under the homological hypothesis. Structurally, narrative shares the characteristics of the sentence without ever being reducible to the simple sum of its sentences: a narrative is a long sentence, just as every constative sentence is in a way the rough outline of a short narrative. Although there provided with different signifiers (often extremely complex), one does find in narrative, expanded and transformed proportionately, the principal verbal categories: tenses, aspects, moods, persons. Moreover the 'subjects' themselves, as opposed to the verbal predicates, readily yield to the sentence model; the actantial typology proposed by A. J. Greimas[2] discovers in the multitude of narrative characters the elementary functions of grammatical analysis. Nor does

1. One of the tasks of such a linguistics would be precisely that of establishing a typology of forms of discourse. Three broad types can be recognized provisionally: metonymic (narrative), metaphoric (lyric poetry, sapiential discourse), enthymematic (intellectual discourse).
2. See below III.1. [Also, section II of 'The struggle with the angel' in the present volume. Greimas's own account can be found in *Sémantique structurale*, Paris 1966, Chapter 10.]

the homology suggested here have merely a heuristic value: it implies an identity between language and literature (inasmuch as the latter can be seen as a sort of privileged vehicle of narrative). It is hardly possible any longer to conceive of literature as an art that abandons all further relation with language the moment it has used it as an instrument to express ideas, passion or beauty: language never ceases to accompany discourse, holding up to it the mirror of its own structure – does not literature, particularly today, make a language of the very conditions of language ?[1]

2. Levels of meaning

From the outset, linguistics furnishes the structural analysis of narrative with a concept which is decisive in that, making explicit immediately what is essential in every system of meaning, namely its organization, it allows us both to show how a narrative is not a simple sum of propositions and to classify the enormous mass of elements which go to make up a narrative. This concept is that of *level of description*.[2]

A sentence can be described, linguistically, on several levels (phonetic, phonological, grammatical, contextual) and these levels are in a hierarchical relationship with one

1. Remember Mallarmé's insight at the time when he was contemplating a work of linguistics: 'Language appeared to him the instrument of fiction: he will follow the method of language (determine it). Language self-reflecting. So fiction seems to him the very process of the human mind – it is this that sets in play all method, and man is reduced to will' *Œuvres complètes*, Bibliothèque de la Pléiade, Paris 1961, p. 851. It will be recalled that for Mallarmé 'Fiction' and 'Poetry' are taken synonymously (cf. ibid., p. 335).

2. 'Linguistic descriptions are not, so to speak, monovalent. A description is not simply "right" or "wrong" in itself . . . it is better thought of as more useful or less', M. A. K. Halliday, 'General linguistics and its application to language teaching', *Patterns of Language*, London 1966, p. 8.

another, for, while all have their own units and correlations (whence the necessity for a separate description of each of them), no level on its own can produce meaning. A unit belonging to a particular level only takes on meaning if it can be integrated in a higher level; a phoneme, though perfectly describable, means nothing in itself: it participates in meaning only when integrated in a word, and the word itself must in turn be integrated in a sentence.[1] The theory of levels (as set out by Benveniste) gives two types of relations: distributional (if the relations are situated on the same level) and integrational (if they are grasped from one level to the next); consequently, distributional relations alone are not sufficient to account for meaning. In order to conduct a structural analysis, it is thus first of all necessary to distinguish several levels or instances of description and to place these instances within a hierarchical (integrationary) perspective.

The levels are operations.[2] It is therefore normal that, as it progresses, linguistics should tend to multiply them. Discourse analysis, however, is as yet only able to work on rudimentary levels. In its own way, rhetoric had assigned at least two planes of description to discourse: *dispositio* and *elocutio*.[3] Today, in his analysis of the structure of myth, Lévi-Strauss has already indicated that the constituent units of mythical discourse (mythemes) acquire meaning only because they are grouped in bundles and because these bundles themselves combine together.[4] As too, Tzvetan

1. The levels of integration were postulated by the Prague School (vid. J. Vachek, *A Prague School Reader in Linguistics*, Bloomington 1964, p. 468) and have been adopted since by many linguists. It is Benveniste who, in my opinion, has given the most illuminating analysis in this respect; op. cit., Chapter 10.

2. 'In somewhat vague terms, a level may be considered as a system of symbols, rules, and so on, to be used for representing utterances', Bach, op. cit., p. 57.

3. The third part of rhetoric, *inventio*, did not concern language – it had to do with *res*, not with *verba*.

4. Claude Lévi-Strauss, *Anthropologie structurale*, Paris 1958, p. 233 [*Structural Anthropology*, New York and London 1963, p. 211].

Todorov, reviving the distinction made by the Russian Formalists, proposes working on two major levels, themselves subdivided: *story* (the argument), comprising a logic of actions and a 'syntax' of characters, and *discourse*, comprising the tenses, aspects and modes of the narrative.[1] But however many levels are proposed and whatever definition they are given, there can be no doubt that narrative is a hierarchy of instances. To understand a narrative is not merely to follow the unfolding of the story, it is also to recognize its construction in 'storeys', to project the horizontal concatenations of the narrative 'thread' on to an implicitly vertical axis; to read (to listen to) a narrative is not merely to move from one word to the next, it is also to move from one level to the next. Perhaps I may be allowed to offer a kind of apologue in this connection. In *The Purloined Letter*, Poe gives an acute analysis of the failure of the chief commissioner of the Paris police, powerless to find the letter. His investigations, says Poe, were perfect *'within the sphere of his speciality'*;[2] he searched everywhere, saturated entirely the level of the 'police search', but in order to find the letter, protected by its conspicuousness, it was necessary to shift to another level, to substitute the concealer's principle of relevance for that of the policeman. Similarly, the 'search' carried out over a horizontal set of narrative relations may well be as thorough as possible but must still, to be effective, also operate 'vertically': meaning is not 'at the end' of the narrative, it runs across it; just as conspicuous as the purloined letter, meaning eludes all unilateral investigation.

1. See T. Todorov, 'Les catégories du récit littéraire', *Communications* 8, 1966 [Todorov's work on narrative is now most easily accessible in two books, *Littérature et Signification*, Paris 1967; *Poétique de la prose*, Paris 1972. For a short account in English, see 'Structural analysis of narrative', *Novel* I, 3, 1969, pp. 70–6].

2. [This in accordance with the Baudelaire version of the Poe story from which Barthes quotes; Poe's original reads: 'so far as his labours extended'.]

A great deal of tentative effort is still required before it will be possible to ascertain precisely the levels of narrative. Those that are suggested in what follows constitute a provisional profile whose merit remains almost exclusively didactic; they enable us to locate and group together the different problems, and this without, I think, being at variance with the few analyses so far.[1] It is proposed to distinguish three levels of description in the narrative work: the level of '*functions*' (in the sense this word has in Propp and Bremond), the level of '*actions*' (in the sense this word has in Greimas when he talks of characters as actants) and the level of '*narration*' (which is roughly the level of 'discourse' in Todorov). These three levels are bound together according to a mode of progressive integration: a function only has meaning insofar as it occupies a place in the general action of an actant, and this action in turn receives its final meaning from the fact that it is narrated, entrusted to a discourse which possesses its own code.

II. Functions

1. The determination of the units

Any system being the combination of units of known classes, the first task is to divide up narrative and determine the segments of narrative discourse that can be distributed into a limited number of classes. In a word, we have to define the smallest narrative units.

Given the integrational perspective described above, the analysis cannot rest satisfied with a purely distributional definition of the units. From the start, meaning must be the criterion of the unit: it is the functional nature of certain segments of the story that makes them units – hence the name 'functions' immediately attributed to these first units.

1. I have been concerned in this introduction to impede research in progress as little as possible.

Since the Russian Formalists,[1] a unit has been taken as any segment of the story which can be seen as the term of a correlation. The essence of a function is, so to speak, the seed that it sows in the narrative, planting an element that will come to fruition later – either on the same level or elsewhere, on another level. If in *Un Cœur simple* Flaubert at one point tells the reader, seemingly without emphasis, that the daughters of the Sous-Préfet of Pont-l'Evêque owned a parrot, it is because this parrot is subsequently to have a great importance in Félicité's life; the statement of this detail (whatever its linguistic form) thus constitutes a function, or narrative unit.

Is everything in a narrative functional? Does everything, down to the slightest detail, have a meaning? Can narrative be divided up entirely into functional units? We shall see in a moment that there are several kinds of functions, there being several kinds of correlations, but this does not alter the fact that a narrative is never made up of anything other than functions: in differing degrees, everything in it signifies. This is not a matter of art (on the part of the narrator), but of structure; in the realm of discourse, what is noted is by definition notable. Even were a detail to appear irretrievably insignificant, resistant to all functionality, it would none-theless end up with precisely the meaning of absurdity or uselessness: everything has a meaning, or nothing has. To put it another way, one could say that art is without noise (as that term is employed in information theory):[2] art is a

1. See especially B. Tomachevski, 'Thématique' (1925), in *Théorie de la littérature* ed. T. Todorov, Paris 1965, pp. 263–307. A little later, Propp defined the function as 'an act of a character, defined from the point of view of its significance for the course of the action' *Morphology of the Folktale*, Austin and London 1968, p. 21.
2. This is what separates art from 'life', the latter knowing only 'fuzzy' or 'blurred' communications. 'Fuzziness' (that beyond which it is impossible to see) can exist in art, but it does so as a coded element (in Watteau for example). Even then, such 'fuzziness' is unknown to the written code: writing is inescapably distinct.

system which is pure, no unit ever goes wasted,[1] however long, however loose, however tenuous may be the thread connecting it to one of the levels of the story.[2]

From the linguistic point of view, the function is clearly a unit of content: it is 'what it says' that makes of a statement a functional unit,[3] not the manner in which it is said. This constitutive signified may have a number of different signifiers, often very intricate. If I am told (in *Goldfinger*) that *Bond saw a man of about fifty*, the piece of information holds simultaneously two functions of unequal pressure: on the one hand, the character's age fits into a certain description of the man (the 'usefulness' of which for the rest of the story is not nil, but diffuse, delayed); while on the other, the immediate signified of the statement is that Bond is unacquainted with his future interlocutor, the unit thus implying a very strong correlation (initiation of a threat and the need to establish the man's identity). In order to determine the initial narrative units, it is therefore vital never to lose sight of the functional nature of the segments under consideration and to recognize in advance that they will not necessarily coincide with the forms into which we traditionally cast the various parts of narrative discourse (actions, scenes, paragraphs, dialogues, interior monologues, etc.) still less with 'psychological' divisions (modes of behaviour,

1. At least in literature, where the freedom of notation (in consequence of the abstract nature of articulated language) leads to a much greater responsibility than in the 'analogical' arts such as cinema.

2. The functionality of a narrative unit is more or less immediate (and hence apparent) according to the level on which it operates: when the units are situated on the same level (as for instance in the case of suspense), the functionality is very clear; it is much less so when the function is saturated on the narrational level – a modern text, weakly signifying on the plane of the anecdote, only finds a full force of meaning on the plane of the writing.

3. 'Syntactical units beyond the sentence are in fact units of content' A. J. Greimas, *Cours de sémantique structurale* (roneoed), 1964, VI, 5 [cf. *Sémantique structurale*, pp. 116f.]. The exploration of the functional level is thus part of general semantics.

feelings, intentions, motivations, rationalizations of characters).

In the same way, since the 'language' ['*langue*'] of narrative is not the language [*langue*] of articulated language [*langage articulé*] – though very often vehicled by it – narrative units will be substantially independent of linguistic units; they may indeed coincide with the latter, but occasionally, not systematically. Functions will be represented sometimes by units higher than the sentence (groups of sentences of varying lengths, up to the work in its entirety) and sometimes by lower ones (syntagm, word and even, within the word, certain literary elements only[1]). When we are told that – the telephone ringing during night duty at Secret Service headquarters – *Bond picked up one of the four receivers*, the moneme *four* in itself constitutes a functional unit, referring as it does to a concept necessary to the story (that of a highly developed bureaucratic technology). In fact, the narrative unit in this case is not the linguistic unit (the word) but only its connoted value (linguistically, the word /four/ never means 'four'); which explains how certain functional units can be shorter than the sentence without ceasing to belong to the order of discourse: such units then extend not beyond the sentence, than which they remain materially shorter, but beyond the level of denotation, which, like the sentence, is the province of linguistics properly speaking.

2. Classes of units

The functional units must be distributed into a small number of classes. If these classes are to be determined without recourse to the substance of content (psychological substance

1. 'The word must not be treated as an indivisible element of literary art, like a brick in building. It can be broken down into much finer "verbal elements"', J. Tynianov, quoted by T. Todorov in *Langages* 6, 1971, p. 18.

for example), it is again necessary to consider the different levels of meaning: some units have as correlates units on the same level, while the saturation of others requires a change of levels; hence, straightaway, two major classes of functions, distributional and integrational. The former correspond to what Propp and subsequently Bremond (in particular) take as functions but they will be treated here in a much more detailed way than is the case in their work. The term *'functions'* will be reserved for these units (though the other units are also functional), the model of description for which has become classic since Tomachevski's analysis: the purchase of a revolver has for correlate the moment when it will be used (and if not used, the notation is reversed into a sign of indecision, etc.); picking up the telephone has for correlate the moment when it will be put down; the intrusion of the parrot into Félicité's home has for correlate the episode of the stuffing, the worshipping of the parrot, etc. As for the latter, the integrational units, these comprise all the *'indices'* (in the very broad sense of the word[1]), the unit now referring not to a complementary and consequential act but to a more or less diffuse concept which is nevertheless necessary to the meaning of the story: psychological indices concerning the characters, data regarding their identity, notations of 'atmosphere', and so on. The relation between the unit and its correlate is now no longer distributional (often several indices refer to the same signified and the order of their occurence in the discourse is not necessarily pertinent) but integrational. In order to understand what an indicial notation 'is for', one must move to a higher level (characters' actions or narration), for only there is the indice clarified: the power of the administrative machine behind Bond, indexed by the number of telephones, has no bearing on the sequence of actions in which Bond is involved by answering the call; it finds its

1. These designations, like those that follow, may all be provisional.

meaning only on the level of a general typology of the actants (Bond is on the side of order). Indices, because of the, in some sort, vertical nature of their relations, are truly semantic units: unlike 'functions' (in the strict sense), they refer to a signified, not to an 'operation'. The ratification of indices is 'higher up', sometimes even remaining virtual, outside any explicit syntagm (the 'character' of a narrative agent may very well never be explicitly named while yet being constantly indexed), is a paradigmatic ratification. That of functions, by contrast, is always 'further on', is a syntagmatic ratification.[1] *Functions* and *indices* thus overlay another classic distinction: functions involve metonymic relata, indices metaphoric relata; the former correspond to a functionality of doing, the latter to a functionality of being.[2]

These two main classes of units, functions and indices, should already allow a certain classification of narratives. Some narratives are heavily functional (such as folktales), while others on the contrary are heavily indicial (such as 'psychological' novels); between these two poles lies a whole series of intermediary forms, dependent on history, society, genre. But we can go further. Within each of the two main classes it is immediately possible to determine two sub-classes of narrative units. Returning to the class of functions, its units are not all of the same 'importance': some constitute real hinge-points of the narrative (or of a fragment of the narrative); others merely 'fill in' the narrative space separating the hinge functions. Let us call the former *cardinal functions* (or *nuclei*) and the latter, having regard to their complementary nature, *catalysers*. For a function to

1. Which does not mean that the syntagmatic setting out of functions may not *finally* hold paradigmatic relations between separate functions, as is recognized since Lévi-Strauss and Greimas.

2. Functions cannot be reduced to actions (verbs), nor indices to qualities (adjectives), for there are actions that are indicial, being 'signs' of a character, an atmosphere, etc.

be cardinal, it is enough that the action to which it refers open (or continue, or close) an alternative that is of direct consequence for the subsequent development of the story, in short that it inaugurate or conclude an uncertainty. If, in a fragment of narrative, *the telephone rings,* it is equally possible to answer or not answer, two acts which will unfailingly carry the narrative along different paths. Between two cardinal functions however, it is always possible to set out subsidiary notations which cluster around one or other nucleus without modifying its alternative nature: the space separating *the telephone rang* from *Bond answered* can be saturated with a host of trivial incidents or descriptions – *Bond moved towards the desk, picked up one of the receivers, put down his cigarette,* etc. These catalysers are still functional, insofar as they enter into correlation with a nucleus, but their functionality is attenuated, unilateral, parasitic; it is a question of a purely chronological functionality (what is described is what separates two moments of the story), whereas the tie between two cardinal functions is invested with a double functionality, at once chronological and logical. Catalysers are only consecutive units, cardinal functions are both consecutive and consequential. Everything suggests, indeed, that the mainspring of narrative is precisely the confusion of consecution and consequence, what comes *after* being read in narrative as what is *caused by*; in which case narrative would be a systematic application of the logical fallacy denounced by Scholasticism in the formula *post hoc, ergo propter hoc* – a good motto for Destiny, of which narrative all things considered is no more than the 'language'.

It is the structural framework of cardinal functions which accomplishes this 'telescoping' of logic and temporality. At first sight, such functions may appear extremely insignificant; what defines them is not their spectacularity (importance, volume, unusualness or force of the narrated action), but, so to speak, the risk they entail: cardinal functions are the risky moments of a narrative. Between these points of alternative, these 'dispatchers', the catalysers lay out areas of safety, rests, luxuries. Luxuries which are not, however, useless: it must be stressed again that from the point of view of the story a catalyser's functionality may be weak but not nil. Were a catalyser purely redundant (in relation to its nucleus), it would nonetheless participate in the economy of the message; in fact, an apparently merely expletive notation always has a discursive function: it accelerates, delays, gives fresh impetus to the discourse, it summarizes, anticipates and sometimes even leads astray.[1] Since what is noted always appears as being notable, the catalyser ceaselessly revives the semantic tension of the discourse, says ceaselessly that there has been, that there is going to be, meaning. Thus, in the final analysis, the catalyser has a constant function which is, to use Jakobson's term, a phatic one:[2] it maintains the contact between narrator and addressee. A nucleus cannot be deleted without altering the story, but neither can a catalyst without altering the discourse.

As for the other main class of units, the indices, an integrational class, its units have in common that they can only be saturated (completed) on the level of characters or on the level of narration. They are thus part of a *parametrical* relation[3] whose second – implicit – term is continuous, extended over an episode, a character or the whole work.

1. Valéry spoke of 'dilatory signs'. The detective novel makes abundant use of such 'confusing' units.

2. [For the scheme of the six factors of verbal communication and their corresponding linguistic functions – emotive, conative, referential, phatic, metalinguistic and poetic – see R. Jakobson, 'Linguistics and Poetics' in *Style in Language*, ed. T. A. Sebeok, New York 1960, pp. 350–77.]

3. N. Ruwet calls 'parametrical' an element which remains constant for the whole duration of a piece of music (for instance, the tempo in a Bach allegro or the monodic character of a solo).

A distinction can be made, however, between *indices* proper, referring to the character of a narrative agent, a feeling, an atmosphere (for example suspicion) or a philosophy, and *informants*, serving to identify, to locate in time and space. To say that through the window of the office where Bond is on duty the moon can be seen half-hidden by thick billowing clouds, is to index a stormy summer night, this deduction in turn forming an index of atmosphere with reference to the heavy, anguish-laden climate of an action as yet unknown to the reader. Indices always have implicit signifieds. Informants, however, do not, at least on the level of the story: they are pure data with immediate signification. Indices involve an activity of deciphering, the reader is to learn to know a character or an atmosphere; informants bring ready-made knowledge, their functionality, like that of catalysers, is thus weak without being nil. Whatever its 'flatness' in relation to the rest of the story, the informant (for example, the exact age of a character) always serves to authenticate the reality of the referent, to embed fiction in the real world. Informants are realist operators and as such possess an undeniable functionality not on the level of the story but on that of the discourse.[1]

Nuclei and catalysers, indices and informants (again, the names are of little importance), these, it seems, are the initial classes into which the functional level units can be divided. This classification must be completed by two remarks. Firstly, a unit can at the same time belong to two different classes: to drink a whisky (in an airport lounge) is an action which can act as a catalyser to the (cardinal) notation of *waiting*, but it is also, and simultaneously, the indice of a

1. In 'Frontières du récit', *Communications* 8, 1966 [reprinted in *Figures II*, Paris 1969], Gérard Genette distinguishes two types of description: ornamental and significant. The second clearly relates to the level of the story; the first to that of the discourse, which explains why for a long time it formed a perfectly coded rhetorical 'piece': *descriptio* or *ekphrasis*, a very highly valued exercise in neo-rhetoric.

certain atmosphere (modernity, relaxation, reminiscence, etc.). In other words, certain units can be mixed, giving a play of possibilities in the narrative economy. In the novel *Goldfinger*, Bond, having to search his adversary's bedroom, is given a master-key by his associate: the notation is a pure (cardinal) function. In the film, this detail is altered and Bond laughingly takes a set of keys from a willing chamber-maid: the notation is no longer simply functional but also indicial, referring to Bond's character (his easy charm and success with women). Secondly, it should be noted (this will be taken up again later) that the four classes just described can be distributed in a different way which is moreover closer to the linguistic model. Catalysers, indices and informants have a common characteristic: in relation to nuclei, they are *expansions*. Nuclei (as will be seen in a moment) form finite sets grouping a small number of terms, are governed by a logic, are at once necessary and sufficient. Once the framework they provide is given, the other units fill it out according to a mode of proliferation in principle infinite. As we know, this is what happens in the case of the sentence, which is made up of simple propositions endlessly complicated with duplications, paddings, embeddings and so on. So great an importance did Mallarmé attach to this type of structure that from it he constructed *Jamais un coup de dés*, a poem which with its 'nodes' and 'loops', its 'nucleus-words' and its 'lace-words', can well be regarded as the emblem of every narrative – of every language.

3. Functional syntax

How, according to what 'grammar', are the different units strung together along the narrative syntagm? What are the rules of the functional combinatory system? Informants and indices can combine freely together: as for example in the portrait which readily juxtaposes data concerning civil status and traits of character. Catalysers and nuclei are linked by a simple relation of implication: a catalyser necessarily implies the existence of a cardinal function to which it can connect, but not vice-versa. As for cardinal functions, they are bound together by a relation of solidarity: a function of this type calls for another function of the same type and reciprocally. It is this last relation which needs to be considered further for a moment – first, because it defines the very framework of the narrative (expansions can be deleted, nuclei cannot); second, because it is the main concern of those trying to work towards a structure of narrative.

It has already been pointed out that structurally narrative institutes a confusion between consecution and consequence, temporality and logic. This ambiguity forms the central problem of narrative syntax. Is there an atemporal logic lying behind the temporality of narrative? Researchers were still quite recently divided on this point. Propp, whose analytic study of the folktale paved the way for the work going on today, is totally committed to the idea of the irreducibility of the chronological order: he sees time as reality and for this reason is convinced of the necessity for rooting the tale in temporality. Yet Aristotle himself, in his contrast between tragedy (defined by the unity of action) and historical narrative (defined by the plurality of actions and the unity of time), was already giving primacy to the logical over the chronological.[1] As do all contemporary researchers (Lévi-Strauss, Greimas, Bremond, Todorov), all of whom (while differing on other points) could subscribe to Lévi-Strauss's proposition that 'the order of chronological succession is absorbed in an atemporal matrix structure'.[2]

1. *Poetics*, 1459a.
2. Quoted by Claude Bremond, 'Le message narratif', *Communications* 4, 1964 [Claude Lévi-Strauss, 'La structure et la forme', *Cahiers*

Analysis today tends to 'dechronologize' the narrative continuum and to 'relogicize' it, to make it dependent on what Mallarmé called with regard to the French language *'the primitive thunderbolts of logic'*;[1] or rather, more exactly (such at least is our wish), the task is to succeed in giving a structural description of the chronological illusion – it is for narrative logic to account for narrative time. To put it another way, one could say that temporality is only a structural category of narrative (of discourse), just as in language [*langue*] temporality only exists in the form of a system; from the point of view of narrative, what we call time does not exist, or at least only exists functionally, as an element of a semiotic system. Time belongs not to discourse strictly speaking but to the referent; both narrative and language know only a semiotic time, 'true' time being a 'realist', referential illusion, as Propp's commentary shows. It is as such that structural analysis must deal with it.[2]

What then is the logic which regulates the principal narrative functions? It is this that current work is actively trying to establish and that has so far been the major focus of debate. Three main directions of research can be seen. The first (Bremond) is more properly logical in approach: it aims to reconstitute the syntax of human behaviour utilized in narrative, to retrace the course of the 'choices' which inevitably face[3] the individual character at every point in

de l'Institut de Science Economique Appliquée 99, March 1960 (Série M, No. 7), p. 29; article reprinted in *Anthropologie structurale II*, Paris 1974].

1. *Œuvres complètes*, p. 386.

2. In his own way – as always perspicacious but left undeveloped – Valéry well expressed the status of narrative time: 'The belief in time as agent and guiding thread is based on *the mechanism of memory and on that of combinatory discourse*', *Tel Quel*, *Œuvres* Vol. II, Bibliothèque de la Pléiade, Paris 1957, p. 348 (my italics); the illusion is precisely produced by the discourse itself.

3. This idea recalls Aristotle: *proairesis*, the rational choice of actions to be undertaken, is the foundation of *praxis*, the practical

the story and so to bring out what could be called an energetic logic,[1] since it grasps the characters at the moment when they choose to act. The second (Lévi-Strauss, Jakobson) is linguistic: its essential concern is to demonstrate paradigmatic oppositions in the functions, oppositions which, in accordance with the Jakobsonian definition of the 'poetic',[2] are 'extended' along the line of the narrative (new developments in Greimas's work correct or complete the conception of the paradigmatic nature of functions[3]). The third (Todorov) is somewhat different in that it sets the analysis at the level of the 'actions' (that is to say, of the characters), attempting to determine the rules by which narrative combines, varies and transforms a certain number of basic predicates.

There is no question of choosing between these working hypotheses; they are not competitive but concurrent, and at present moreover are in the throes of elaboration. The only complement we will attempt to give them here concerns the dimensions of the analysis. Even leaving aside the indices, informants and catalysers, there still remains in a narrative (especially if it is a novel and no longer a tale) a very large number of cardinal functions and many of these cannot be mastered by the analyses just mentioned, which until now have worked on the major articulations of narrative. Provision needs to be made, however, for a description

---

science which, contrary to *poiesis*, produces no object-work distinct from its agent. Using these terms, one can say that the analyst tries to reconstitute the praxis inherent in narrative.

1. Such a logic, based on alternatives (*doing this or that*), has the merit of accounting for the process of dramatization for which narrative is usually the occasion.

2. ['The poetic function projects the principle of equivalence of the axis of selection on to the axis of combination.' Jakobson, 'Linguistics and Poetics', p. 3.]

3. See A. J. Greimas, 'Eléments pour une théorie de l'interprétation du récit mythique', *Communications* 8, 1966 [article reprinted in *Du Sens*, Paris 1970].

sufficiently close as to account for *all* the narrative units, for the smallest narrative segments. We must remember that cardinal functions cannot be determined by their 'importance', only by the (doubly implicative) nature of their relations. A 'telephone call', no matter how futile it may seem, on the one hand itself comprises some few cardinal functions (telephone ringing, picking up the receiver, speaking, putting down the receiver), while on the other, taken as a whole, it must be linkable – at the very least proceeding step by step – to the major articulations of the anecdote. The functional covering of the narrative necessitates an organization of relays the basic unit of which can only be a small group of functions, hereafter referred to (following Bremond) as a *sequence*.

A sequence is a logical succession of nuclei bound together by a relation of solidarity:[1] the sequence opens when one of its terms has no solidary antecedent and closes when another of its terms has no consequent. To take a deliberately trivial example, the different functions order a drink, obtain it, drink it, pay for it, constitute an obviously closed sequence, it being impossible to put anything before the order or after the payment without moving out of the homogeneous group *'Having a drink'*. The sequence indeed is always nameable. Determining the major functions of the folktale, Propp and subsequently Bremond have been led to name them (*Fraud, Betrayal, Struggle, Contract, Seduction*, etc.); the naming operation is equally inevitable in the case of trivial sequences, the 'micro-sequences' which often form the finest grain of the narrative tissue. Are these namings solely the province of the analyst? In other words, are they purely metalinguistic? No doubt they are, dealing as they do with the code of narrative. Yet at the same time they can be imagined as forming part of an inner meta-

1. In the Hjelmslevian sense of double implication: two terms presuppose one another.

language in the reader (or listener) him who grasps every logical succession of actions as a nominal whole: to read is to name; to listen is not only to perceive a language, it is also to construct it. Sequence titles are similar enough to the *cover-words* of translation machines which acceptably cover a wide variety of meanings and shades of meaning. The narrative language [*la langue du récit*] within us comprises from the start these essential headings: the closing logic which structures a sequence is inextricably linked to its name; any function which initiates a *seduction* prescribes from the moment it appears, in the name to which it gives rise, the entire process of seduction such as we have learned it from all the narratives which have fashioned in us the language of narrative.

However minimal its importance, a sequence, since it is made up of a small number of nuclei (that is to say, in fact, of 'dispatchers'), always involves moments of risk and it is this which justifies analysing it. It might seem futile to constitute into a sequence the logical succession of trifling acts which go to make up the offer of a cigarette (*offering, accepting, lighting, smoking*), but precisely, at every one of these points, an alternative – and hence a freedom of meaning – is possible. Du Pont, Bond's future partner, offers him a light from his lighter but Bond refuses; the meaning of this bifurcation is that Bond instinctively fears a booby-trapped gadget.[1] A sequence is thus, one can say, a *threatened logical unit*, this being its justification *a minimo*. It is also founded *a maximo*: enclosed on its function, subsumed under a name, the sequence itself constitutes a new unit, ready to function as a simple term in another, more extensive se-

1. It is quite possible to identify even at this infinitesimal level an opposition of paradigmatic type, if not between two terms, at least between two poles of the sequence: the sequence *Offer of a cigarette* spreads out, by suspending it, the paradigm *Danger/Safety* (demonstrated by Cheglov in his analysis of the Sherlock Holmes cycle), *Suspicion/Protection, Aggressiveness/Friendliness*.

quence. Here, for example, is a micro-sequence: *hand held out, hand shaken, hand released*. This *Greeting* then becomes a simple function: on the one hand, it assumes the role of an indice (flabbiness of Du Pont, Bond's distaste); on the other, it forms globally a term in a larger sequence, with the name *Meeting*, whose other terms (*approach, halt, interpellation, sitting down*) can themselves be micro-sequences. A whole network of subrogations structures the narrative in this way, from the smallest matrices to the largest functions. What is in question here, of course, is a hierarchy that remains within the functional level: it is only when it has been possible to widen the narrative out step by step, from Du Pont's cigarette to Bond's battle against Goldfinger, that functional analysis is over – the pyramid of functions then touches the next level (that of the Actions). There is both a syntax within the sequences and a (subrogating) syntax between the sequences together. The first episode of *Goldfinger* thus takes on a 'stemmatic' aspect:

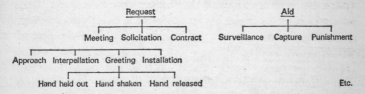

Obviously this representation is analytical; the reader perceives a linear succession of terms. What needs to be noted, however, is that the terms from several sequences can easily be imbricated in one another: a sequence is not yet completed when already, cutting in, the first term of a new sequence may appear. Sequences move in counterpoint;[1] functionally, the structure of narrative is fugued: thus it

1. This counterpoint was recognized by the Russian Formalists who outlined its typology; it is not without recalling the principal 'intricate' structures of the sentence (see below V.I.).

is this that narrative at once 'holds' and 'pulls on'. Within the single work, the imbrication of sequences can indeed only be allowed to come to a halt with a radical break if the sealed-off blocks which then compose it are in some sort recuperated at the higher level of the Actions (of the characters). *Goldfinger* is composed of three functionally independent episodes, their functional stemmas twice ceasing to intercommunicate: there is no sequential relation between the swimming-pool episode and the Fort Knox episode; but there remains an actantial relation, for the characters (and consequently the structure of their relations) are the same. One can recognize here the epic pattern (a 'whole made of multiple fables'): the epic is a narrative broken at the functional level but unitary at the actantial level (something which can be verified in the *Odyssey* or in Brecht's plays). The level of functions (which provides the major part of the narrative syntagm) must thus be capped by a higher level from which, step by step, the first level units draw their meaning, the level of actions.

III. Actions

1. Towards a structural status of characters

In Aristotelian poetics, the notion of character is secondary, entirely subsidiary to the notion of action: there may be actions without 'characters', says Aristotle, but not characters without an action; a view taken over by classical theoreticians (Vossius). Later the character, who until then had been only a name, the agent of an action,[1] acquired a psychological consistency, became an individual, a 'person', in short a fully constituted 'being', even should he do nothing and of course even before acting.[2] Characters

1. It must not be forgotten that classical tragedy as yet knows only 'actors', not 'characters'.
2. The 'character-person' reigns in the bourgeois novel; in *War and*

stopped being subordinate to the action, embodied immediately psychological essences; which essences could be drawn up into lists, as can be seen in its purest form in the list of 'character parts' in bourgeois theatre (the coquette, the noble father, etc.). From its very outset, structural analysis has shown the utmost reluctance to treat the character as an essence, even merely for purposes of classification; Tomachevski went so far as to deny the character any narrative importance, a point of view he subsequently modified. Without leaving characters out of the analysis altogether, Propp reduced them to a simple typology based not on psychology but on the unity of the actions assigned them by the narrative (*Donor of a magical agent, Helper, Villain,* etc.).

Since Propp, the character has constantly set the structural analysis of narrative the same problem. On the one hand, the characters (whatever one calls them – *dramatis personae* or *actants*) form a necessary plane of description, outside of which the slightest reported 'actions' cease to be intelligible; so that it can be said that there is not a single narrative in the world without 'characters',[1] or at least without agents. Yet on the other hand, these – extremely numerous – 'agents' can be neither described nor classified in terms of 'persons' – whether the 'person' be considered as a purely historical form, limited to certain genres (those most familiar to us it is true), in which case it is necessary to leave out of account the very large number of narratives

---

Peace, Nikolay Rostov is from the start a good fellow, loyal, courageous and passionate, Prince Andrey a disillusioned individual of noble birth, etc. What happens illustrates them, it does not form them.

1. If one section of contemporary literature has attacked the 'character', it is not in order to destroy it (which is impossible) but to depersonalize it, which is quite different. A novel seemingly devoid of characters, such as *Drame* by Philippe Sollers, gets rid of the person to the benefit of language but nonetheless retains a fundamental play of actants confronting the very action of discourse. There is still a 'subject' in this literature, but that 'subject' is henceforth that of language.

(popular tales, modern texts) comprising agents but not persons, or whether the 'person' is declared to be no more than a critical rationalization foisted by our age on pure narrative agents. Structural analysis, much concerned not to define characters in terms of psychological essences, has so far striven, using various hypotheses, to define a character not as a 'being' but as a 'participant'. For Bremond, every character (even secondary) can be the agent of sequences of actions which belong to him (*Fraud*, *Seduction*); when a single sequence involves two characters (as is usual), it comprises two perspectives, two names (what is *Fraud* for the one is *Gullibility* for the other); in short, every character (even secondary) is the hero of his own sequence. Todorov, analysing a 'psychological' novel (*Les Liaisons dangereuses*), starts not from the character-persons but from the three major relationships in which they can engage and which he calls base predicates (love, communication, help). The analysis brings these relationships under two sorts of rules: rules of *derivation*, when it is a question of accounting for other relationships, and rules of *action*, when it is a question of describing the transformation of the major relationships in the course of the story. There are many characters in *Les Liaisons dangereuses* but 'what is said of them' (their predicates) can be classified. Finally, Greimas has proposed to describe and classify the characters of narrative not according to what they are but according to what they do (whence the name *actants*), inasmuch as they participate in three main semantic axes (also to be found in the sentence: subject, object, indirect object, adjunct) which are communication, desire (or quest) and ordeal.[1] Since this participation is ordered in couples, the infinite world of characters is, it too, bound by a paradigmatic structure (*Subject/Object*, *Donor/Receiver*, *Helper/Opponent*) which is projected along the narrative; and since

1. *Sémantique structurale*, pp. 129f.

an actant defines a class, it can be filled by different actors, mobilized according to rules of multiplication, substitution or replacement.

These three conceptions have many points in common. The most important, it must be stressed again, is the definition of the character according to participation in a sphere of actions, these spheres being few in number, typical and classifiable; which is why this second level of description, despite its being that of the characters, has here been called the level of Actions: the word *actions* is not to be understood in the sense of the trifling acts which form the tissue of the first level but in that of the major articulations of *praxis* (desire, communication, struggle).

2. The problem of the subject

The problems raised by a classification of the characters of narrative are not as yet satisfactorily resolved. Certainly there is ready agreement on the fact that the innumerable characters of narrative can be brought under rules of substitution and that, even within the one work, a single figure can absorb different characters.[1] Again, the actantial model proposed by Greimas (and adopted by Todorov in another perspective) seems to stand the test of a large number of narratives. Like any structural model, its value lies less in its canonic form (a matrix of six actants) than in the regulated transformations (replacements, confusions, duplications, substitutions) to which it lends itself, thus holding out the hope of an actantial typology of narratives.[2] A difficulty,

1. Psychoanalysis has widely accredited these operations of condensation. Mallarmé was saying already, writing of *Hamlet*: 'Supernumeraries, necessarily! for in the ideal painting of the stage, everything moves according to a symbolic reciprocity of types amongst themselves or relatively to a single figure.' *Crayonné au théâtre, Œuvres complètes,* p. 301.

2. For example: narratives where object and subject are confounded

however, is that when the matrix has a high classificational power (as is the case with Greimas's actants) it fails adequately to account for the multiplicity of participations as soon as these are analysed in terms of perspectives and that when these perspectives are respected (as in Bremond's description) the system of characters remains too fragmented. The reduction proposed by Todorov avoids both pitfalls but has so far only been applied to one narrative. All this, it seems, can be quickly and harmoniously resolved. The real difficulty posed by the classification of characters is the place (and hence the existence) of the *subject* in any actantial matrix, whatever its formulation. *Who* is the subject (the hero) of a narrative? Is there – or not – a privileged class of actors? The novel has accustomed us to emphasize in one way or another – sometimes in a devious (negative) way – one character in particular. But such privileging is far from extending over the whole of narrative literature. Many narratives, for example, set two adversaries in conflict over some stake; the subject is then truly double, not reducible further by substitution. Indeed, this is even perhaps a common archaic form, as though narrative, after the fashion of certain languages, had also known a *dual* of persons. This dual is all the more interesting in that it relates narrative to the structures of certain (very modern) games in which two equal opponents try to gain possession of an object put into circulation by a referee; a schema which recalls the actantial matrix proposed by Greimas, and there is nothing surprising in this if one is willing to allow that a game, being a language, depends on the same symbolic structure as is to be found in language and narrative: a game too is

---

in a single character, that is narratives of the search for oneself, for one's own identity (*The Golden Ass*); narratives where the subject pursues successive objects (*Madame Bovary*), etc.

a sentence.[1] If therefore a privileged class of actors is retained (the subject of the quest, of the desire, of the action), it needs at least to be made more flexible by bringing that actant under the very categories of the grammatical (and not psychological) person. Once again, it will be necessary to look towards linguistics for the possibility of describing and classifying the personal (*je/tu*, first person/second person) or apersonal (*il*, third person), singular, dual or plural, instance of the action. It will – perhaps – be the grammatical categories of the person (accessible in our pronouns) which will provide the key to the actional level; but since these categories can only be defined in relation to the instance of discourse, not to that of reality,[2] characters, as units of the actional level, find their meaning (their intelligibility) only if integrated in the third level of description, here called the level of Narration (as opposed to Functions and Actions).

IV. Narration

1. Narrative communication

Just as there is within narrative a major function of exchange (set out between a donor and a beneficiary), so, homologically, narrative as object is the point of a communication: there is a donor of the narrative and a receiver of the narrative. In linguistic communication, *je* and *tu* (*I* and *you*) are absolutely presupposed by one another; similarly, there can be no narrative without a narrator and a listener (or reader). Banal perhaps, but still little developed. Certainly the role of the sender has been abundantly enlarged upon (much study of the 'author' of a novel, though

1. Umberto Eco's analysis of the James Bond cycle ('James Bond: une combinatoire narrative', *Communications* 8, 1966) refers more to game than to language.

2. See the analyses of person given by Benveniste in *Problèmes de linguistique générale*.

without any consideration of whether he really is the 'narrator'); when it comes to the reader, however, literary theory is much more modest. In fact, the problem is not to introspect the motives of the narrator or the effects the narration produces on the reader, it is to describe the code by which narrator and reader are signified throughout the narrative itself. At first sight, the signs of the narrator appear more evident and more numerous than those of the reader (a narrative more frequently says *I* than *you*); in actual fact, the latter are simply more oblique than the former. Thus, each time the narrator stops 'representing' and reports details which he knows perfectly well but which are unknown to the reader, there occurs, by signifying failure, a sign of reading, for there would be no sense in the narrator giving himself a piece of information. *Leo was the owner of the joint*,[1] we are told in a first-person novel: a sign of the reader, close to what Jakobson calls the conative function of communication. Lacking an inventory however, we shall leave aside for the moment these signs of reception (though they are of equal importance) and say a few words concerning the signs of narration.[2]

Who is the donor of the narrative? So far, three conceptions seem to have been formulated. The first holds that a narrative emanates from a person (in the fully psychological sense of the term). This person has a name, the author, in whom there is an endless exchange between the 'personality' and the 'art' of a perfectly identified individual who periodically takes up his pen to write a story: the narrative (notably the novel) then being simply the expression of an *I*

1. *Double Bang à Bangkok* [secret agent thriller by Jean Bruce, Paris 1959]. The sentence functions as a 'wink' to the reader, as if he was being turned towards. By contrast, the statement '*So Leo had just left*' is a sign of the narrator, part of a process of reasoning conducted by a 'person'.

2. In 'Les catégories du récit littéraire' Todorov deals with the images of narrator and reader.

external to it. The second conception regards the narrator as a sort of omniscient, apparently impersonal, consciousness that tells the story from a superior point of view, that of God:[1] the narrator is at once inside his characters (since he knows everything that goes on in them) and outside them (since he never identifies with any one more than another). The third and most recent conception (Henry James, Sartre) decrees that the narrator must limit his narrative to what the characters can observe or know, everything proceeding as if each of the characters in turn were the sender of the narrative. All three conceptions are equally difficult in that they seem to consider narrator and characters as real – 'living' – people (the unfailing power of this literary myth is well known), as though a narrative were originally determined at its referential level (it is a matter of equally 'realist' conceptions). Narrator and characters, however, at least from our perspective, are essentially 'paper beings'; the (material) author of a narrative is in no way to be confused with the narrator of that narrative.[2] The signs of the narrator are immanent to the narrative and hence readily accessible to a semiological analysis; but in order to conclude that the author himself (whether declared, hidden or withdrawn) has 'signs' at his disposal which he sprinkles through his work, it is necessary to assume the existence between this 'person' and his language of a straight descriptive relation which makes the author a full subject and and the narrative the instrumental expression of that fullness. Structural analysis is unwilling to accept such an assumption: *who speaks* (in the narrative)

1. 'When will someone write from the point of view of a *superior joke*, that is as God sees things from above?' Flaubert, *Préface à la vie d'écrivain*, ed. G. Bollème, Paris 1965, p. 91.
2. A distinction all the more necessary, given the scale at which we are working, in that historically a large mass of narratives are without authors (oral narratives, folktales, epics entrusted to bards, reciters, tc.).

is not *who writes* (in real life) and *who writes* is not *who is*.[1]

In fact, narration strictly speaking (the code of the narrator), like language, knows only two systems of signs: personal and apersonal. These two narrational systems do not necessarily present the linguistic marks attached to person (*I*) and non-person (*he*): there are narratives or at least narrative episodes, for example, which though written in the third person nevertheless have as their true instance the first person. How can we tell? It suffices to rewrite the narrative (or the passage) from *he* to *I*: so long as the rewriting entails no alteration of the discourse other than this change of the grammatical pronouns, we can be sure that we are dealing with a personal system. The whole of the beginning of *Goldfinger*, though written in the third person, is in fact 'spoken' by James Bond. For the instance to change, rewriting must become impossible; thus the sentence 'he saw a man in his fifties, still young-looking . . .' is perfectly personal despite the *he* ('I, James Bond, saw . . .'), but the narrative statement 'the tinkling of the ice against the glass appeared to give Bond a sudden inspiration' cannot be personal on account of the verb 'appeared', it (and not the *he*) becoming a sign of the apersonal. There is no doubt that the apersonal is the traditional mode of narrative, language having developed a whole tense system peculiar to narrative (based on the aorist[2]), designed to wipe out the present of the speaker. As Benveniste puts it: 'In narrative, no one speaks.' The personal instance (under more or less disguised forms) has, however, gradually invaded narrative, the narration being referred to the *hic et nunc* of the locutionary act (which is the definition of the personal system). Thus it is that today many narratives

1. J. Lacan: 'Is the subject I speak of when I speak the same as the subject who speaks?'
2. E. Benveniste, op. cit. [especially Chapter XIX].

are to be found (and of the most common kinds) which mix together in extremely rapid succession, often within the limits of a single sentence, the personal and the apersonal; as for instance this sentence from *Goldfinger*:

His eyes,	*personal*
grey-blue,	*apersonal*
looked into those of Mr Du Pont who did not know what face to put on	*personal*
for this look held a mixture of candour, irony and self-deprecation.	*apersonal*

The mixing of the systems is clearly felt as a facility and this facility can go as far as trick effects. A detective novel by Agatha Christie (*The Sittaford Mystery*) only keeps the enigma going by cheating on the person of the narration: a character is described from within when he is already the murderer[1] – as if in a single person there were the consciousness of a witness, immanent to the discourse, and the consciousness of a murderer, immanent to the referent, with the dishonest tourniquet of the two systems alone producing the enigma. Hence it is understandable that at the other pole of literature the choice of a rigorous system should have been made a necessary condition of a work – without it always being easy fully to meet that condition.

Rigour of this kind – the aim of certain contemporary writers – is not necessarily an aesthetic imperative. What is called the psychological novel usually shows a mixture of the two systems, successively mobilizing the signs of non-person and those of person; 'psychology', that is, paradoxically, cannot accommodate itself to a pure system, for by bringing the whole narrative down to the sole instance of the discourse – or, if one prefers, to the locutionary

1. Personal mode: 'It even seemed to Burnaby that nothing looked changed . . .' The device is still more blatant in *The Murder of Roger Ackroyd*, since there the murderer actually says *I*.

act – it is the very content of the person which is threatened:
the psychological person (of referential order) bears no
relation to the linguistic person, the latter never defined by
states of mind, intentions or traits of character but only by
its (coded) place in discourse. It is this formal person that
writers today are attempting to speak and such an attempt
represents an important subversion (the public moreover
has the impression that 'novels' are no longer being written)
for it aims to transpose narrative from the purely constative plane, which it has occupied until now, to the performative plane, whereby the meaning of an utterance is the very
act by which it is uttered:[1] today, writing is not 'telling'
but saying that one is telling and assigning all the referent
('what one says') to this act of locution; which is why part
of contemporary literature is no longer descriptive, but
transitive, striving to accomplish so pure a present in its
language that the whole of the discourse is identified with
the act of its delivery, the whole *logos* being brought down
– or extended – to a *lexis*.[2]

2. Narrative situation

The narrational level is thus occupied by the signs of narrativity, the set of operators which reintegrate functions
and actions in the narrative communication articulated on
its donor and its addressee. Some of these signs have already
received study; we are familiar in oral literatures with certain
codes of recitation (metrical formulae, conventional
presentation protocols) and we know that here the 'author'
is not the person who invents the finest stories but the person

1. On the performative, see Todorov's 'Les catégories du récit
littéraire'. The classic example of a performative is the statement *I
declare war* which neither 'constates' nor 'describes' anything but
exhausts its meaning in the act of its utterance (by contrast to the
statement *the king declared war*, which constates, describes).
2. For the opposition logos/lexis, see Genette, 'Frontières du récit'.

who best masters the code which is practised equally by his listeners: in such literatures the narrational level is so clearly defined, its rules so binding, that it is difficult to conceive of a 'tale' devoid of the coded signs of narrative (*'once upon a time'*, etc.). In our written literatures, the 'forms of discourse' (which are in fact signs of narrativity) were early identified: classification of the modes of authorial intervention (outlined by Plato and developed by Diomedes[1]), coding of the beginnings and endings of narratives, definition of the different styles of representation (*oratio directa, oratio indirecta* with its *inquit, oratio tecta*),[2] study of 'points of view' and so on. All these elements form part of the narrational level, to which must obviously be added the writing as a whole, its role being not to 'transmit' the narrative but to display it.

It is indeed precisely in a display of the narrative that the units of the lower levels find integration: the ultimate form of the narrative, as narrative, transcends its contents and its strictly narrative forms (functions and actions). This explains why the narrational code should be the final level attainable by our analysis, other than by going outside of the narrative-object, other, that is, than by transgressing the rule of immanence on which the analysis is based. Narration can only receive its meaning from the world which makes use of it: beyond the narrational level begins the world, other systems (social, economic, ideological) whose terms are no longer simply narratives but elements of a different substance (historical facts, determinations, behaviours, etc.). Just as linguistics stops at the sentence, so narrative analysis stops at discourse – from there it is

1. *Genus activum vel imitativum* (no intervention of the narrator in the discourse: as for example theatre); *genus ennarativum* (the poet alone speaks: sententiae, didactic poems); *genus commune* (mixture of the two kinds: epic poems).

2. H. Sorensen in *Language and Society* (Studies presented to Jansen), p. 150.

necessary to shift to another semiotics. Linguistics is acquainted with such boundaries which it has already postulated – if not explored – under the name of *situations*. Halliday defines the 'situation' (in relation to a sentence) as 'the associated non-linguistic factors',[1] Prieto as 'the set of facts known by the receiver at the moment of the semic act and independently of this act'.[2] In the same way, one can say that every narrative is dependent on a 'narrative situation', the set of protocols according to which the narrative is 'consumed'. In so-called 'archaic' societies, the narrative situation is heavily coded;[3] nowadays, avant-garde literature alone still dreams of reading protocols – spectacular in the case of Mallarmé who wanted the book to be recited in public according to a precise combinatory scheme, typographical in that of Butor who tries to provide the book with its own specific signs. Generally, however, our society takes the greatest pains to conjure away the coding of the narrative situation: there is no counting the number of narrational devices which seek to naturalize the subsequent narrative by feigning to make it the outcome of some natural circumstance and thus, as it were, 'dis-inaugurating' it: epistolary novels, supposedly rediscovered manuscripts, author who met the narrator, films which begin the story before the credits. The reluctance to declare its codes characterizes bourgeois society and the mass culture issuing from it: both demand signs which do not look like signs. Yet this is only, so to speak, a structural epiphenomenon: however familiar, however casual may today be the act of opening a novel or a newspaper or of turning on the television, nothing can prevent that humble

1. M. A. K. Halliday, op. cit., p. 4.
2. L. J. Prieto, *Principes de noologie*, Paris and The Hague 1964, p. 36.
3. A tale, as Lucien Sebag stressed, can be told anywhere anytime, but not a mythical narrative.

act from installing in us, all at once and in its entirety, the narrative code we are going to need. Hence the narrational level has an ambiguous role: contiguous to the narrative situation (and sometimes even including it), it gives on to the world in which the narrative is undone (consumed), while at the same time, capping the preceding levels, it closes the narrative, constitutes it definitively as utterance of a language [*langue*] which provides for and bears along its own metalanguage.

V. The System of Narrative

Language [*langue*] proper can be defined by the concurrence of two fundamental processes: articulation, or segmentation, which produces units (this being what Benveniste calls *form*), and integration, which gathers these units into units of a higher rank (this being *meaning*). This dual process can be found in the language of narrative [*la langue du récit*] which also has an articulation and an integration, a form and a meaning.

1. Distortion and expansion

The form of narrative is essentially characterized by two powers: that of distending its signs over the length of the story and that of inserting unforeseeable expansions into these distortions. The two powers appear to be points of freedom but the nature of narrative is precisely to include these 'deviations' within its language.[1]

The distortion of signs exists in linguistic language [*langue*] and was studied by Bally with reference to French

1. Valéry: 'Formally the novel is close to the dream; both can be defined by consideration of this curious property: *all their deviations form part of them.*'

and German.[1] Dystaxia occurs when the signs (of a message) are no longer simply juxtaposed, when the (logical) linearity is disturbed (predicate before subject for example). A notable form of dystaxia is found when the parts of one sign are separated by other signs along the chain of the message (for instance, the negative *ne jamais* and the verb *a pardonné* in *elle ne nous a jamais pardonné*): the sign split into fractional parts, its signified is shared out amongst several signifiers, distant from one another and not comprehensible on their own. This, as was seen in connection with the functional level, is exactly what happens in narrative: the units of a sequence, although forming a whole at the level of that very sequence, may be separated from one another by the insertion of units from other sequences – as was said, the structure of the functional level is fugued.[2] According to Bally's terminology, which opposes synthetic languages where dystaxia is predominant (such as German) and analytic languages with a greater respect for logical linearity and monosemy (such as French), narrative would be a highly synthetic language, essentially founded on a syntax of embedding and enveloping: each part of the narrative radiates in several directions at once. When Bond orders a whisky while waiting for his plane, the whisky as indice has a polysemic value, is a kind of symbolic node grouping several signifieds (modernity, wealth, leisure); as a functional unit, however, the ordering of the whisky has to run step by step through numerous relays (consumption, waiting, departure, etc.) in order to find its final meaning: the unit is 'taken' by the whole narrative at the same time that the narrative only 'holds' by the distortion and

1. Charles Bally, *Linguistique générale et linguistique française*, Paris 1932.
2. Cf. Lévi-Strauss: 'Relations pertaining to the same bundle may appear diachronically at remote intervals' *Anthropologie structurale*, p. 234 [trans. p. 211]. A. J. Greimas has emphasized the spacing out of functions.

irradiation of its units.

This generalized distortion is what gives the language of narrative its special character. A purely logical phenomenon, since founded on an often distant relation and mobilizing a sort of confidence in intellective memory, it ceaselessly substitutes meaning for the straightforward copy of the events recounted. On meeting in 'life', it is most unlikely that the invitation to take a seat would not immediately be followed by the act of sitting down; in narrative these two units, contiguous from a mimetic point of view, may be separated by a long series of insertions belonging to quite different functional spheres. Thus is established a kind of *logical time* which has very little connection with real time, the apparent pulverization of units always being firmly held in place by the logic that binds together the nuclei of the sequence. 'Suspense' is clearly only a privileged – or 'exacerbated' – form of distortion: on the one hand, by keeping a sequence open (through emphatic procedures of delay and renewal), it reinforces the contact with the reader (the listener), has a manifestly phatic function; while on the other, it offers the threat of an uncompleted sequence, of an open paradigm (if, as we believe, every sequence has two poles), that is to say, of a logical disturbance, it being this disturbance which is consumed with anxiety and pleasure (all the more so because it is always made right in the end). 'Suspense', therefore, is a game with structure, designed to endanger and glorify it, constituting a veritable 'thrilling' of intelligibility: by representing order (and no longer series) in its fragility, 'suspense' accomplishes the very idea of language: what seems the most pathetic is also the most intellectual – 'suspense' grips you in the 'mind', not in the 'guts'.[1]

1. J. P. Faye, writing of Klossowski's *Baphomet*: 'Rarely has fiction (or narrative) so clearly revealed what it always is, necessarily: an experimentation of "thought" on "life".' *Tel Quel* 22, p. 88.

What can be separated can also be filled. Distended, the functional nuclei furnish intercalating spaces which can be packed out almost infinitely; the interstices can be filled in with a very large number of catalysers. Here, however, a new typology comes in, for the freedom to catalyse can be regulated according both to the content of the functions (certain functions are more apt than others for catalysing – as for example *Waiting*[1]) and to the substance of the narrative (writing contains possibilities of diaeresis – and so of catalysing – far superior to those of film: a gesture related linguistically can be 'cut up' much more easily than the same gesture visualized[2]). The catalystic power of narrative has for corollary its elliptic power. Firstly, a function (*he had a good meal*) can economize on all the potential catalysers it covers over (the details of the meal)[3]; secondly, it is possible to reduce a sequence to its nuclei and a hierarchy of sequences to its higher terms without altering the meaning of the story: a narrative can be identified even if its total syntagm be reduced to its actants and its main functions as these result from the progressive upwards integration of its functional units.[4] In other words, narrative lends itself to *summary* (what used to be called the *argument*). At first sight this is true of any discourse, but each discourse has its own kind of summary. A lyric poem, for example, is simply the

1. Logically *Waiting* has only two nuclei: 1. the wait established 2. the wait rewarded or disappointed; the first, however, can be extensively catalysed, occasionally even indefinitely (*Waiting for Godot*): yet another game – this time extreme – with structure.

2. Valéry: 'Proust divides up – and gives us the feeling of being able to divide up indefinitely – what other writers are in the habit of passing over.'

3. Here again, there are qualifications according to substance: literature has an unrivalled elliptic power – which cinema lacks.

4. This reduction does not necessarily correspond to the division of the book into chapters; on the contrary, it seems that increasingly chapters have the role of introducing breaks, points of suspense (serial technique).

vast metaphor of a single signified[1] and to summarize it is thus to give this signified, an operation so drastic that it eliminates the poem's identity (summarized, lyric poems come down to the signifieds *Love* and *Death*) – hence the conviction that poems cannot be summarized. By contrast, the summary of a narrative (if conducted according to structural criteria) preserves the individuality of the message; narrative, in other words, is *translatable* without fundamental damage. What is untranslatable is determined only at the last, narrational, level. The signifiers of narrativity, for instance, are not readily transferable from novel to film, the latter utilizing the personal mode of treatment only very exceptionally;[2] while the last layer of the narrational level, namely the writing, resists transference from one language to another (or transfers very badly). The translatability of narrative is a result of the structure of its language, so that it would be possible, proceeding in reverse, to determine this structure by identifying and classifying the (varyingly) translatable and untranslatable elements of a narrative. The existence (now) of different and concurrent semiotics (literature, cinema, comics, radio-television) would greatly facilitate this kind of analysis.

2. Mimesis and meaning

The second important process in the language of narrative

1. N. Ruwet: 'A poem can be understood as the outcome of a series of transformations applied to the proposition "I love you".' 'Analyse structurale d'un poème français', *Linguistics* 3, 1964, p. 82. Ruwet here refers precisely to the analysis of paranoiac delirium given by Freud in connection with President Schreber ('Psychoanalytic Notes on an Autobiographical Account of a Case of Paranoia', *Standard Edition* Vol. 12).

2. Once again, there is no relation between the grammatical 'person' of the narrator and the 'personality' (or subjectivity) that a film director puts into his way of presenting a story: the *camera-I* (continuously identified with the vision of a particular character) is exceptional in the history of cinema.

is integration: what has been disjoined at a certain level (a sequence for example) is most often joined again at a higher level (a hierarchically important sequence, the global signified of a number of scattered indices, the action of a class of characters). The complexity of a narrative can be compared to that of an organization profile chart, capable of integrating backwards and forwards movements; or, more accurately, it is integration in various forms which compensates for the seemingly unmasterable complexity of units on a particular level. Integration guides the understanding of the discontinuous elements, simultaneously contiguous and heterogeneous (it is thus that they appear in the syntagm which knows only one dimension – that of succession). If, with Greimas, we call *isotopy* the unity of meaning (that, for instance, which impregnates a sign and its context), then we can say that integration is a factor of isotopy: each (integrational) level gives its isotopy to the units of the level below, prevents the meaning from 'dangling' – inevitable if the staggering of levels were not perceived. Narrative integration, however, does not present itself in a serenely regular manner like some fine architectural style leading by symmetrical chicaneries from an infinite variety of simple elements to a few complex masses. Very often a single unit will have two correlates, one on one level (function of a sequence), the other on another (indice with reference to an actant). Narrative thus appears as a succession of tightly interlocking mediate and immediate elements; dystaxia determines a 'horizontal' reading, while integration superimposes a 'vertical' reading: there is a sort of structural 'limping', an incessant play of potentials whose varying falls give the narrative its dynamism or energy: each unit is perceived at once in its surfacing and in its depth and it is thus that the narrative 'works'; through the concourse of these two movements the structure ramifies, proliferates, uncovers itself – and recovers itself, pulls itself together:

the new never fails in its regularity. There is, of course, a freedom of narrative (just as there is a freedom for every speaker with regard to his or her language), but this freedom is limited, literally *hemmed in*: between the powerful code of language [*langue*] and the powerful code of narrative a hollow is set up – the sentence. If one attempts to embrace the whole of a written narrative, one finds that it starts from the most highly coded (the phonematic, or even the merismatic, level), gradually relaxes until it reaches the sentence, the farthest point of combinatorial freedom, and then begins to tighten up again, moving progressively from small groups of sentences (micro-sequences), which are still very free, until it comes to the main actions, which form a strong and restricted code. The creativity of narrative (at least under its mythical appearance of 'life') is thus situated *between two codes*, the linguistic and the trans-linguistic. That is why it can be said paradoxically that *art* (in the Romantic sense of the term) is a matter of statements of detail, whereas *imagination* is mastery of the code: 'It will be found in fact,' wrote Poe, 'that the ingenious are always fanciful, and the *truly* imaginative never otherwise than analytic . . .'[1]

Claims concerning the 'realism' of narrative are therefore to be discounted. When a telephone call comes through in the office where he is on duty, Bond, so the author tells us, reflects that 'Communications with Hong-Kong are as bad as they always were and just as difficult to obtain'. Neither Bond's 'reflection' nor the poor quality of the telephone call is the real piece of information; this contingency perhaps gives things more 'life' but the true information, which will come to fruition later, is the localization of the telephone call, Hong-Kong. In all narrative imitation remains contingent.[2] The function of narrative is not to 'represent', it

1. *The Murders in the Rue Morgue.*
2. G. Genette rightly reduces *mimesis* to passages of directly

is to constitute a spectacle still very enigmatic for us but in any case not of a mimetic order. The 'reality' of a sequence lies not in the 'natural' succession of the actions composing it but in the logic there exposed, risked and satisfied. Putting it another way, one could say that the origin of a sequence is not the observation of reality, but the need to vary and transcend the first *form* given man, namely repetition: a sequence is essentially a whole within which nothing is repeated. Logic has here an emancipatory value – and with it the entire narrative. It may be that men ceaselessly re-inject into narrative what they have known, what they have experienced; but if they do, at least it is in a form which has vanquished repetition and instituted the model of a process of becoming. Narrative does not show, does not imitate; the passion which may excite us in reading a novel is not that of a 'vision' (in actual fact, we do not 'see' anything). Rather it is that of meaning, that of a higher order of relation which also has its emotions, its hopes, its dangers, its triumphs. 'What takes place' in a narrative is from the referential (reality) point of view literally *nothing*;[1] 'what happens' is language alone, the adventure of language, the unceasing celebration of its coming. Although we know scarcely more about the origins of narrative than we do about the origins of language, it can reasonably be suggested that narrative is contemporaneous with monologue, a creation seemingly posterior to that of dialogue. At all events, without wanting to strain the phylogenetic hypothesis, it may be significant that it is at the same moment (around the age of three) that the little human 'invents' at once sentence, narrative, and the Oedipus.

---

reported dialogue (cf. 'Frontières du récit'); yet even dialogue always contains a function of intelligibility, not of mimesis.

1. Mallarmé: 'A dramatic work displays the succession of exteriors of the act without any moment retaining reality and, in the end, anything happening.' *Crayonné au théâtre, Œuvres complètes*, p. 296.

The Struggle with the Angel

Textual analysis of Genesis 32: 22–32

(22) And he rose up that night, and took his two wives, and his two women-servants, and his eleven sons, and passed over the ford Jabbok. (23) And he took them, and sent them over the brook, and sent over that he had. (24) And Jacob was left alone; and there wrestled a man with him until the breaking of the day. (25) And when he saw that he prevailed not against him, he touched the hollow of his thigh; and the hollow of Jacob's thigh was out of joint as he wrestled with him. (26) And he said, Let me go, for the day breaketh. And he said, I will not let thee go, except thou bless me. (27) And he said unto him, What is thy name? And he said, Jacob. (28) And he said, Thy name shall be called no more Jacob, but Israel: for as a prince hast thou power with God and with men, and hast prevailed. (29) And Jacob asked him, and said, Tell me, I pray thee, thy name. And he said, Wherefore is it thou dost ask after my name? And he blessed him there. (30) And Jacob called the name of the place Peniel: for I have seen God face to face, and my life is preserved. (31) And as he passed over Penuel the sun rose upon him, and he halted upon his thigh. (32) Therefore the children of Israel eat not of the sinew which shrank, which is upon the hollow of the thigh, unto this day: because he touched the hollow of Jacob's thigh in the sinew that shrank. (*Authorized Version*)

The clarifications – or precautionary remarks – which will serve as an introduction to the following analysis will in fact be largely negative. First of all, it must be said that I shall not be giving any preliminary exposition of the principles, perspectives and problems of the structural analysis of narrative. That analysis is not a science nor even a discipline (it is not taught), but, as part of the newly developing semiology, it nevertheless represents an area of research which is becoming well known, so much so that to set out its prolegomena on the occasion of every fresh analysis[1] would be to run the risk of producing an impression of useless repetition. Moreover, the structural analysis presented here will not be very pure. I shall indeed be referring in the main to the principles shared by all those semiologists concerned with narrative and, to finish, I shall even show how the piece under discussion lends itself to an extremely classic and almost canonical structural analysis, this orthodox consideration (orthodox from the point of view of the structural analysis of narrative) is all the more justified in that we shall be dealing with a mythical narrative that may have entered writing (entered Scripture) via an oral tradition. At the same time, however, I shall allow myself every so often (and perhaps continuously on the quiet) to direct my investigations towards an analysis with which I am more at home, textual analysis ('textual' is used with reference to the contemporary theory of the *text*, this being understood as production of *signifiance* and not as philological object, custodian of the Letter). Such an analysis endeavours to 'see' each particular text in its difference – which does not mean in its ineffable individuality, for this difference is 'woven' in familiar codes; it conceives the text as taken up in an *open* network which is the very infinity of language, itself structured without closure; it tries to say no longer *from where* the text comes (historical criticism), nor even

1. On this subject (and in relation to exegesis), see R. Barthes, 'L'analyse structurale du récit: à propos d'*Actes* 10–11', in *Exégèse et Herméneutique*, Paris 1971, pp. 181–204.

how it is made (structural analysis), but how it is unmade, how it explodes, disseminates – by what coded paths it *goes off*. Finally, the last of these precautionary remarks and intended to forestall any disappointment, there is no question in what follows of a methodological confrontation between structural or textual analysis and exegesis, this lying outside my competence.[1] I shall simply analyse the text of *Genesis 32* (traditionally called 'Jacob's struggle with the angel') as though I were at the first stage of a piece of research (which is indeed the case). What is given here is not a 'result' nor even a 'method' (which would be too ambitious and would imply a 'scientific' view of the text that I do not hold), but merely a 'way of proceeding'.

I. Sequential Analysis

Structural analysis embraces roughly three types or three objects of analysis, or again, if one prefers, comprises three tasks. 1) The inventorization and classification of the 'psychological', biographical, characterial and social attributes of the characters involved in the narrative (age, sex, external qualities, social situation or position of importance, etc.). Structurally, this is the area of indices (notations, of infinitely varied expression, serving to transmit a signified – as, for example, 'irritability', 'grace', 'strength' – which the analyst names in his metalanguage; it being understood that the metalinguistic term may very well not figure directly in the text – as indeed is generally the case – which will not employ 'irritability' or 'grace' or whatever. If

1. I wish to express my gratitude to Jean Alexandre whose socio-historical, linguistic and exegetical knowledge, together with his intellectual openness, helped me to understand the text analysed here. Many of his ideas are to be found in this analysis and only fear of having distorted them has prevented me from acknowledging them each time they appear.

one establishes a homology between narrative and (the linguistic) sentence, then the indice corresponds to the adjective, to the *epithet* (which, let us not forget, was a figure of rhetoric). This is what we might call *indicial analysis*. 2) The inventorization and classification of the *functions* of the characters; what they do according to their narrative status, in their capacity as subject of an action that remains constant: the Sender, the Seeker, the Emissary, etc. In terms of the sentence, this would be the equivalent of the *present participle* and is that *actantial analysis* of which A. J. Greimas was the first to provide the theory. 3) The inventorization and classification of the *actions*, the plane of the *verbs*. These narrative actions are organized in sequences, in successions apparently ordered according to a pseudo-logical schema (it is a matter of a purely empirical, cultural logic, a product of experience – even if ancestral – and not of reasoning). What we have here is thus *sequential analysis*.

Our text lends itself, if in fact briefly, to indicial analysis. The contest it describes can be read as an indice of Jacob's strength (attested in other episodes of the chronicle of this hero's exploits) and that indice leads towards an anagogical meaning which is the (invincible) strength of God's Elect. Actantial analysis is also possible, but as the text is essentially made up of seemingly contingent actions it is better to work mainly on a sequential (or actional) analysis of the episode, being prepared in conclusion to add one or two remarks concerning the actantial. I shall divide the text (without, I think, forcing things) into three sequences: 1. the Crossing, 2. the Struggle, 3. the Namings.

1. *The Crossing* (v. 22–24). Let us straightaway give the schema of the sequences of this episode, a schema which is twofold or at least, as it were, 'strabismic' (what is at stake here will be seen in a moment):

I

II

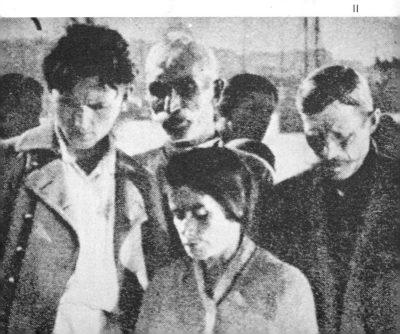

III

IV

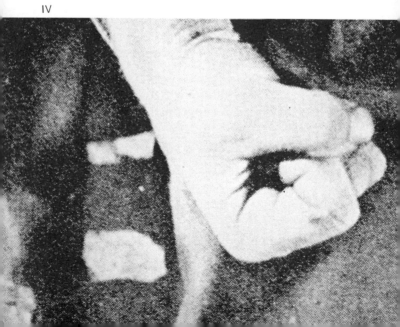

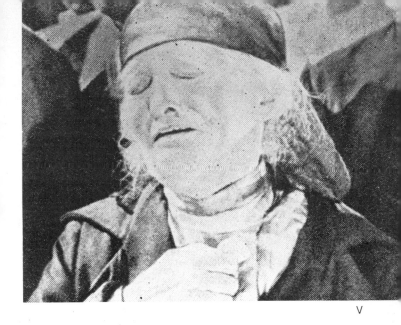

V

VI

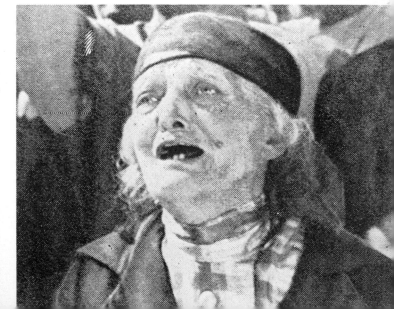

VII

VIII

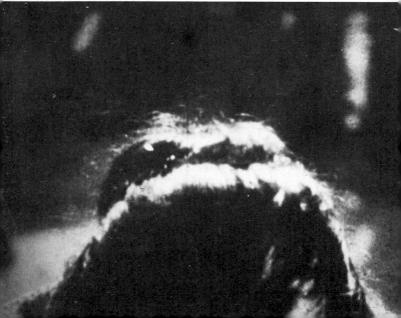

IX

X

XI

XII

XIII

XIV

XV

XVI

XVII

PATES - SAUCE - PARMESAN
A L'ITALIENNE DE LUXE

I   rise up   gather together   pass over
       22   22   22

II   gather together   send over   remain alone
            23   23   24

It can be noted at once that structurally *rise up* is a simple *operator for beginning*; one might say, putting things quickly, that by *rise up* is to be understood not only that Jacob starts moving but also that the discourse *gets underway*. The beginning of a narrative, of a discourse, of a text, is an extremely sensitive point – *where to begin?* The *said* must be torn from the *not-said*, whence a whole rhetoric of beginning *markers*. The most important thing, however, is that the two sequences (or sub-sequences) seem to be in a state of redundancy (which is perhaps usual in the discourse of the period: a piece of information is given and then repeated; but the rule here is reading, not the historical and philological determination of the text: we are reading the text not in its 'truth' but in its 'production' – which is not its 'determination'). Paradoxically moreover (for redundancy habitually serves to homogenize, to clarify and assure a message), when read after two millennia of Aristotelian rationalism (Aristotle being the principal theoretician of classic narrative) the redundancy of the two sub-sequences creates an abrasion, a grating of readability. The sequential schema, that is, can be read in two ways: 1) Jacob himself crosses over the ford – if need be after having made several trips back and forth – and thus the combat takes place on the left bank of the flood (he is coming from the North) *after he has definitively crossed over*; in this case, *send over* is read *cross over himself*; 2) Jacob sends over but does not himself cross over; he fights on the right bank of the

Jabbok *before crossing over*, in a rearguard position. Let
us not look for some *true* interpretation (perhaps our very
hesitation will appear ridiculous in the eyes of the exegetes);
rather, let us consume two different pressures of readability:
1) if Jacob remains alone *before* crossing the Jabbok, we are
led towards a 'folkloric' reading of the episode, the mythical
reference then being overwhelming which has it that a trial
of strength (as for example with a dragon or the guardian
spirit of a river) must be imposed on the hero *before* he
clears the obstacle, *so that* – once victorious – he can clear it;
2) if on the contrary Jacob having crossed over (he and his
tribe), he remains alone on the good side of the flood
(the side of the country to which he wants to go), then the
passage is without structural finality while acquiring on the
other hand a religious finality: if Jacob is alone, it is no
longer to settle the question of and obtain the crossing but
in order that he be *marked* with solitude (the familiar *setting
apart* of the one chosen by God). There is a historical
circumstance which increases the undecidability of the
two interpretations. Jacob's purpose is to return home, to
enter the land of Canaan: given this, the crossing of the
River Jordan would be easier to understand than that of
the Jabbok. In short, we are confronted with the crossing of
a spot that is neutral. The crossing is crucial if Jacob has
to win it over the guardian of the place, indifferent if what
is important is the solitude, the mark of Jacob. Perhaps
we have here the tangled trace of two stories, or at least of
two narrative instances: the one, more 'archaic' (in the
simple stylistic sense of the term), makes of the crossing
itself an ordeal; the other, more 'realist', gives a 'geographical' air to Jacob's journey by mentioning the places
he goes through (without attaching any mythical value to
them).

If one carries back on to this twofold sequence the pattern
of subsequent events, that is the Struggle and the Naming,

the dual reading continues, coherent to the end in each of its two versions. Here again is the diagram:

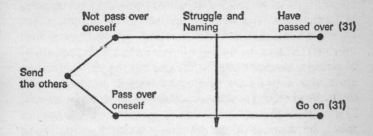

If the Struggle stands between the 'not pass over' and the 'have passed over' (the folklorizing, mythical reading), then the mutation of the Names corresponds to the very purpose of every etymological saga; if on the contrary the Struggle is only a stage between a position of immobility (of meditation, of election) and a movement of setting off again, then the mutation of the Name has the value of a spiritual rebirth (of 'baptism'). All of which can be summarized by saying that in this first episode there is sequential readability but cultural ambiguity. No doubt the theologian would grieve at this indecision while the exegete would acknowledge it. hoping for some element of fact or argument that would enable him to put an end to it. The textual analyst, judging by my own impression, savours such *friction* between two intelligibilities.

2. *The Struggle* (v. 24–29). For the second episode we have once again to start from a complication (which is not to say a doubt) of readability – remember that textual analysis is founded on *reading* rather than on the objective structure of the text, the latter being more the province of structural analysis. This complication stems from the interchangeable character of the pronouns which refer to the

two opponents in the combat: a style which a purist would describe as *muddled* but whose lack of sharpness doubtless posed no problem for Hebrew syntax. Who is 'a man'? Staying within verse 25, is it 'a man' who does not succeed in getting the better of Jacob or Jacob who cannot prevail over this someone? Is the 'he' of 'he prevailed not against him' (25) the same as the 'he' of 'And he said' (26)? Assuredly everything becomes clear in the end but it requires in some sort a retroactive reasoning of a syllogistic kind: you have vanquished God. He who is speaking to you is he whom you vanquished. Therefore he who is speaking to you is God. The identification of the opponents is oblique, the readability is *diverted* (whence occasionally commentaries which border on total misunderstanding; as for example: 'He wrestles with the Angel of the Lord and, thrown to the ground, obtains from him the certainty that God is with him').

Structurally, this amphibology, even if subsequently clarified, is not without significance. It is not in my opinion (which is, I repeat, that of a reader today) a simple complication of expression due to an unpolished, archaizing style; it is bound up with a paradoxical structure of the contest (paradoxical when compared with the stereotypes of mythical combat). So as to appreciate this paradox in its structural subtlety, let us imagine for a moment an endoxical (and no longer paradoxical) reading of the episode: A wrestles with B but fails to get the better of him; to gain victory at all costs, A then resorts to some exceptional strategy, whether an unfair and forbidden blow (the forearm chop in wrestling matches) or a blow which, while remaining within the rules, supposes a secret knowledge, a 'dodge' (the 'ploy' of the Jarnac blow[1]). *In the very logic of the narrative* such a blow, generally described as 'decisive', brings victory to the

1. [In 1547 Guy de Jarnac won a duel by an unexpected thrust which hamstrung his opponent.]

person who administers it: the emphatic mark of which this blow is structurally the object cannot be reconciled with its being ineffective – by the very god of narrative it *must* succeed. Here, however, the opposite occurs: the decisive blow fails; A, who gave the blow, is not the victor; which is the structural paradox. The sequence then takes an unexpected course:

Combat (durative)	Powerlessness of A	Decisive blow	(Ineffectiveness)	Negotiation
24	25	25		26

	A's request	Bargaining	Acceptance
	26	26	29

It will be noted that A (it matters little from the point of view of the structure if this be *someone, a man, God* or *the Angel*) is not strictly speaking vanquished but *held in check*. For this to be seen as a defeat, the adjunction of a *time limit* is needed: this is the breaking of day ('for the day breaketh' 26), a notation which picks up verse 24 ('until the breaking of day') but now in the explicit context of a mythical structure. The theme of the nocturnal combat is structurally justified by the fact that at a certain moment, fixed in advance (as is the rising of the sun, as is the duration of a boxing match), the rules of the combat will no longer obtain, the structural play will come to an end, as too the supernatural play (the 'demons' withdraw at dawn). Thus we can see that it is within a quite 'regular' combat that the sequence sets up an unexpected readability, a logical surprise: the person who has the knowledge, the secret, the special ploy, is nevertheless defeated. The sequence itself, however actional, however anecdotal it may be, functions to *unbalance* the opponents in the combat, not only by the unforeseen victory of the one over the other, but above all (let us be fully aware of the *formal* subtlety of this surprise) by the illogical, *inverted*, nature of the victory. In other words (and here we find an eminently structural term, well known to linguists), the combat, as it is reversed in its unexpected development, *marks* one of the combatants: the weakest defeats the strongest, *in exchange for which* he is marked (on the thigh).

It is plausible (moving somewhat away from pure structural analysis and approaching textual analysis, vision *without barriers* of meanings) to fill out this schema of the mark (of the disequilibrium) with contents of an ethnological kind. The structural meaning of the episode, once again, is the following: a situation of balance (the combat at its outset) – and such a situation is a prerequisite for any marking (ascesis in Ignatius of Loyola for instance functions to establish the *indifference* of the will which allows the manifestation of the divine mark, the choice, the election) – is disturbed by the unlikely victory of one of the participants: there is an inversion of the mark, a counter-mark. Let us turn then to the family configuration. Traditionally, the line of brothers is in principle evenly balanced (they are all situated on the same level in relation to the parents); this equality of birth is normally unbalanced by the right of primogeniture: the eldest is marked. Now in the story of Jacob, there is an inversion of the mark, a counter-mark: it is the younger who supplants the elder (*Genesis* 27: 36), taking his brother by the heel in order to reverse time; it is Jacob, the younger brother, who marks himself. Since Jacob has just obtained a mark in his struggle with God, one can say in a sense that A (God) is the substitute of the elder brother, once again beaten by the younger. The conflict with Esau is *displaced* (every symbol is a *displacement*; if the 'struggle with the angel' is symbolic, then it has displaced something). Commentary – for which I am insufficiently equipped – would at this point doubtless have to widen the interpretation of the *inversion of the mark*, by placing it either in a historico-economic context – Esau is the eponym of the Edomites and there were economic ties between the Edomites and the Israelites; figured here perhaps is an overthrow of the alliance, the start of a new league of interests? – or in the field of the symbolic (in the psychoanalytical sense of the term) – the Old Testament seems to be less the world of the Fathers than that of the Enemy Brothers, the elder are ousted in favour of the younger; in the myth of the Enemy Brothers Freud pointed to the theme of *the smallest difference*: is not the blow on the thigh, on the thin sinew, just such a *smallest difference?* Be that as it may, in this world God marks the young, acts against nature: his (structural) function is to constitute a *counter-marker*.

To conclude discussion of this extremely rich episode of the Struggle, of the Mark, I should like to add a remark as semiologist. We have seen that in the binary opposition of the combatants, which is perhaps the binary opposition of the Brothers, the younger is marked both by the reversal of the anticipated distribution of strengths and by a bodily sign, the touch on the thigh, the halting (not without re-calling Oedipus, Swollen Foot, the Lame One). A mark is creative of meaning. In the phonological representation of language, the 'equality' of the paradigm is unbalanced in favour of a marked element by the presence of a trait absent from its correlative and oppositional term. By marking Jacob (Israel), God (or the Narrative) permits an anagogical development of meaning, creates the formal operational conditions of a new 'language', the election of Israel being its 'message'. God is a logothete, a founder of a language, and Jacob is here a 'morpheme' of the new language.

3. *The Namings or Mutations* (v. 27–32). The object of the

final sequence is the exchange of names, that is to say the promotion of new statuses, new powers. Naming is clearly related to Blessing: to bless (to accept the homage of a kneeling suppliant) and to name are both suzerain acts. There are two namings:

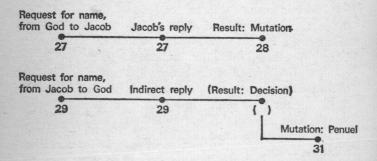

The mutation bears on Names, but in fact it is the entire episode which functions as *the creation of a multiple trace* – across Jacob's body, the status of the Brothers, Jacob's name of the place, the kind of food (creation of an alimentary taboo: the whole story can also be interpreted *a minimo* as the mythical foundation of a taboo). The three sequences that have been analysed are homological; what is in question in each is a *change* – of place, parental line, name, alimentary rite; all this keeping very close to an activity of language, a transgression of the rules of meaning.

Such is the sequential (or actional) analysis of our text. As has been seen, I have tried to remain always on the level of the structure, that is to say of the systematic correlation of the terms denoting an action. If I have chanced to mention certain possible meanings, the purpose has not been to discuss the probability of those meanings but rather to show how the structure 'disseminates' contents – which each reading can make its own. My object is not the philological or historical document, custodian of a truth to be discovered, but the volume, the *signifiance* of the text.

II. Structural Analysis

The structural analysis of narrative being in part already constituted (by Propp, Lévi-Strauss, Greimas, Bremond), I wish to conclude – putting myself even more in the background – by confronting the text under discussion with two modes of structural analysis so as to demonstrate the interest of these two modes, though my own work has a somewhat different orientation:[1] Greimas's actantial analysis and Propp's functional analysis.

1. *Actantial analysis.* The actantial grid worked out by Greimas[2] – to be used, as he himself says, with prudence and flexibility – divides the characters, the actors, of a narrative into six formal classes of actants, defined by what they do according to narrative status and not by what they are psychologically (thus one actant may combine several characters just as a single character may combine several actants; an actant may also be figured by an inanimate entity). The 'struggle with the angel' forms a very familiar episode in mythical narratives: the overcoming of an obstacle, the Ordeal. As far as the particular episode is concerned (things might perhaps be different over the whole set of Jacob's exploits), the actants are 'filled' as follows: Jacob is the *Subject* (subject of the demand, the quest, the action); the *Object* (of the same demand, quest, action) is the crossing of the guarded and forbidden place, the flood, the Jabbok; the *Sender*, who sets in circulation the stake of the quest (namely the crossing of the flood), is obviously God; the *Receiver* is Jacob again (two actants are here

1. My work on Balzac's story *Sarrasine* (*S/Z*, Paris 1970; [trans. *S/Z*, New York and London 1975]) belongs more to textual than to structural analysis.
2. See especially A. J. Greimas, *Sémantique structurale* and *Du Sens*.

present in a single figure); the *Opponent* (the one or ones who hinder the Subject in his quest) is God himself (it is he who, mythically, guards the crossing); the *Helper* (the one or ones who aid the Subject) is Jacob who provides help to himself through his own, legendary, strength (an indicial trait, as was noted).

The paradox, or at very least the anomic nature of the formulation, can be seen at once: that the subject be confounded with the receiver is banal; that the subject be his or her own helper is less usual (it generally occurs in 'voluntarist' narratives or novels); but that the sender be the opponent is very rare and there is only one type of narrative that can present this paradoxical form – narratives relating an act of blackmail. If the opponent were only the (provisional) holder of the stake, then of course there would be nothing extraordinary: it is the opponent's role to have and defend ownership of the object that the hero wants to obtain (as with the dragon guarding a place to be crossed). Here however, as in every blackmail, God, at the same time that he guards the flood, also dispenses the mark, the privilege. The actantial form of the text is thus far from conciliatory: structurally, it is extremely audacious – which squares well with the 'scandal' represented by God's defeat.

2. *Functional analysis.* Propp was the first to establish the structure of the folktale, by dividing it into its *functions* or narrative acts.[1] The functions, according to Propp, are stable elements, limited in number (some thirty or so) and always identical in their concatenation, even if occasionally certain functions are absent from this or that narrative. It so happens – as will be seen in a moment –

1. V. Propp, *Morphology of the Folktale*. Unfortunately, the word 'function' is always ambiguous; at the beginning of the present piece we used it to define actantial analysis which assesses characters by their roles in the action (precisely their 'function'); in Propp's terminology, there is a shift from character to the action itself, grasped in its *relations* to the actions surrounding it.

that our text fulfills perfectly a section of the functional schema brought to light by Propp who would have been unable to imagine a more convincing application of his discovery.

In a preparatory section of the folktale (as analysed by Propp) there necessarily occurs an absence of the hero, something already the case in the tale of Jacob. Isaac sends Jacob far from his homeland to Laban (*Genesis* 28: 2 and 5). Our episode effectively begins at the fifteenth of Propp's narrative functions and can be coded in the following manner, showing at each stage the striking parallelism between Propp's schema and the *Genesis* narrative:

Propp and the folktale	*Genesis*
15. Transference from one place to another (by bird, horse, ship, etc.)	Set out from the North, from the Aramaeans, from the house of Laban, Jacob journeys home, to his father's house (29: 1, Jacob sets out)
16. Combat between the Villain and the Hero	This is the sequence of the Struggle (32: 24–27)
17. The hero is branded, 'marked' (generally it is a matter of a mark on the body, but in other cases it is simply the gift of a jewel, of a ring)	Jacob is marked on the thigh (32: 25–32)
18. Victory of the Hero, defeat of the Villain	Jacob's victory (32: 26)
19. Liquidation of the misfortune or lack: the misfortune or lack had been established in the initial absence of the Hero: this absence is repaired	Having succeeded in crossing Penuel (32: 31), Jacob reaches Schechem in Canaan (33: 18)

There are other parallels. In Propp's function 14, the hero acquires the use of a magical object; for Jacob this talisman is obviously the blessing that he surprises his blind father into giving him (*Genesis* 27). Again, function 29 represents the transfiguration of the hero (for example, the Beast transformed into a handsome nobleman); such a transfiguration seems to be present in the changing of the Name (*Genesis* 32: 28) and the rebirth it implies. The narrative model stamps God with the role of the Villain (his *structural* role – it is not a question of a psychological role); the fact is that a veritable folktale stereotype can be read in the *Genesis* episode – the difficult crossing of a ford guarded by a hostile spirit. A further similitude between episode and tale is that in both cases character motivations (their reasons for acting) go unnoted, the ellipsis of such notations being not a stylistic element but a pertinent structural characteristic of the narration. Structural analysis in the strict sense of the term would thus conclude emphatically that the 'struggle with the angel' is a true fairytale, since according to Propp all fairytales belong to the same structure, the one he described.

So we can see that what might be called the structural exploitation of the episode is very possible and even imperative. Let me indicate in conclusion, however, that what interests me most in this famous passage is not the 'folkloristic' model but the abrasive frictions, the breaks, the discontinuities of readability, the juxtaposition of narrative entities which to some extent run free from an explicit logical articulation. One is dealing here (this at least is for me the savour of the reading) with a sort of *metonymic montage*: the themes (Crossing, Struggle, Naming, Alimentary Rite) are *combined*, not 'developed'. This abruptness, this asyndetic character of the narrative is well expressed by Hosea (12: 3–4):

'He took his brother by the heel in the womb / / and by his strength he had power with God.'

Metonymic logic is that of the unconscious. Hence it is perhaps in that direction that one would need to pursue the present study, to pursue the reading of the text – its dissemination, not its truth. Evidently, there is a risk in so doing of weakening the episode's economico-historical force (certainly existent, at the level of the exchanges of tribes and the questions of power). Yet equally in so doing the symbolic explosion of the text (not necessarily of a religious order) is reinforced. The problem, the problem at least posed for me, is exactly to manage not to reduce the Text to a signified, whatever it may be (historical, economic, folkloristic or kerygmatic), but to hold its *signifiance* fully open.

The Death of the Author

In his story *Sarrasine* Balzac, describing a castrato disguised as a woman, writes the following sentence: *'This was woman herself, with her sudden fears, her irrational whims, her instinctive worries, her impetuous boldness, her fussings, and her delicious sensibility.'* Who is speaking thus? Is it the hero of the story bent on remaining ignorant of the castrato hidden beneath the woman? Is it Balzac the individual, furnished by his personal experience with a philosophy of Woman? Is it Balzac the author professing 'literary' ideas on femininity? Is it universal wisdom? Romantic psychology? We shall never know, for the good reason that writing is the destruction of every voice, of every point of origin. Writing is that neutral, composite, oblique space where our subject slips away, the negative where all identity is lost, starting with the very identity of the body writing.

No doubt it has always been that way. As soon as a fact is *narrated* no longer with a view to acting directly on reality but intransitively, that is to say, finally outside of any function other than that of the very practice of the symbol itself, this disconnection occurs, the voice loses its origin, the author enters into his own death, writing begins. The sense of this phenomenon, however, has varied; in ethnographic societies the responsibility for a narrative is never assumed by a person but by a mediator, shaman or relator whose 'performance' – the mastery of the narrative code – may possibly be admired but never his 'genius'. The author is a modern figure, a product of our society insofar as, emerging from the Middle Ages with English empiricism,

French rationalism and the personal faith of the Reformation, it discovered the prestige of the individual, of, as it is more nobly put, the 'human person'. It is thus logical that in literature it should be this positivism, the epitome and culmination of capitalist ideology, which has attached the greatest importance to the 'person' of the author. The *author* still reigns in histories of literature, biographies of writers, interviews, magazines, as in the very consciousness of men of letters anxious to unite their person and their work through diaries and memoirs. The image of literature to be found in ordinary culture is tyrannically centred on the author, his person, his life, his tastes, his passions, while criticism still consists for the most part in saying that Baudelaire's work is the failure of Baudelaire the man, Van Gogh's his madness, Tchaikovsky's his vice. The *explanation* of a work is always sought in the man or woman who produced it, as if it were always in the end, through the more or less transparent allegory of the fiction, the voice of a single person, the *author* 'confiding' in us.

Though the sway of the Author remains powerful (the new criticism has often done no more than consolidate it), it goes without saying that certain writers have long since attempted to loosen it. In France, Mallarmé was doubtless the first to see and to foresee in its full extent the necessity to substitute language itself for the person who until then had been supposed to be its owner. For him, for us too, it is language which speaks, not the author; to write is, through a prerequisite impersonality (not at all to be confused with the castrating objectivity of the realist novelist), to reach that point where only language acts, 'performs', and not 'me'. Mallarmé's entire poetics consists in suppressing the author in the interests of writing (which is, as will be seen, to restore the place of the reader). Valéry, encumbered by a psychology of the Ego, considerably diluted Mallarmé's

theory but, his taste for classicism leading him to turn to
the lessons of rhetoric, he never stopped calling into question
and deriding the Author; he stressed the linguistic and, as it
were, 'hazardous' nature of his activity, and throughout his
prose works he militated in favour of the essentially verbal
condition of literature, in the face of which all recourse to
the writer's interiority seemed to him pure superstition.
Proust himself, despite the apparently psychological
character of what are called his *analyses*, was visibly concerned with the task of inexorably blurring, by an extreme
subtilization, the relation between the writer and his
characters; by making of the narrator not he who has seen
and felt nor even he who is writing, but he who *is going to
write* (the young man in the novel – but, in fact, how old is
he and who is he? – wants to write but cannot; the novel
ends when writing at last becomes possible), Proust gave
modern writing its epic. By a radical reversal, instead of
putting his life into his novel, as is so often maintained,
he made of his very life a work for which his own book was
the model; so that it is clear to us that Charlus does not
imitate Montesquiou but that Montesquiou – in his anecdotal, historical reality – is no more than a secondary
fragment, derived from Charlus. Lastly, to go no further
than this prehistory of modernity, Surrealism, though
unable to accord language a supreme place (language being
system and the aim of the movement being, romantically,
a direct subversion of codes – itself moreover illusory:
a code cannot be destroyed, only 'played off'), contributed
to the desacrilization of the image of the Author by ceaselessly recommending the abrupt disappointment of expecta-
tions of meaning (the famous surrealist 'jolt'), by entrusting
the hand with the task of writing as quickly as possible
what the head itself is unaware of (automatic writing), by
accepting the principle and the experience of several people
writing together. Leaving aside literature itself (such dis-

tinctions really becoming invalid), linguistics has recently provided the destruction of the Author with a valuable analytical tool by showing that the whole of the enunciation is an empty process, functioning perfectly without there being any need for it to be filled with the person of the interlocutors. Linguistically, the author is never more than the instance writing, just as *I* is nothing other than the instance saying *I*: language knows a 'subject', not a 'person', and this subject, empty outside of the very enunciation which defines it, suffices to make language 'hold together', suffices, that is to say, to exhaust it.

The removal of the Author (one could talk here with Brecht of a veritable 'distancing', the Author diminishing like a figurine at the far end of the literary stage) is not merely an historical fact or an act of writing; it utterly transforms the modern text (or – which is the same thing – the text is henceforth made and read in such a way that at all its levels the author is absent). The temporality is different. The Author, when believed in, is always conceived of as the past of his own book: book and author stand automatically on a single line divided into a *before* and an *after*. The Author is thought to *nourish* the book, which is to say that he exists before it, thinks, suffers, lives for it, is in the same relation of antecedence to his work as a father to his child. In complete contrast, the modern scriptor is born simultaneously with the text, is in no way equipped with a being preceding or exceeding the writing, is not the subject with the book as predicate; there is no other time than that of the enunciation and every text is eternally written *here and now*. The fact is (or, it follows) that *writing* can no longer designate an operation of recording, notation, representation, 'depiction' (as the Classics would say); rather, it designates exactly what linguists, referring to Oxford philosophy, call a performative, a rare verbal form (exclusively given in the first person and in the present tense) in which the enunciation has no other content (contains no other proposition) than the act by which it is uttered – something like the *I declare* of kings or the *I sing* of very ancient poets. Having buried the Author, the modern scriptor can thus no longer believe, as according to the pathetic view of his predecessors, that this hand is too slow for his thought or passion and that consequently, making a law of necessity, he must emphasize this delay and indefinitely 'polish' his form. For him, on the contrary, the hand, cut off from any voice, borne by a pure gesture of inscription (and not of expression), traces a field without origin – or which, at least, has no other origin than language itself, language which ceaselessly calls into question all origins.

We know now that a text is not a line of words releasing a single 'theological' meaning (the 'message' of the Author-God) but a multi-dimensional space in which a variety of writings, none of them original, blend and clash. The text is a tissue of quotations drawn from the innumerable centres of culture. Similar to Bouvard and Pécuchet, those eternal copyists, at once sublime and comic and whose profound ridiculousness indicates precisely the truth of writing, the writer can only imitate a gesture that is always anterior, never original. His only power is to mix writings, to counter the ones with the others, in such a way as never to rest on any one of them. Did he wish to *express himself*, he ought at least to know that the inner 'thing' he thinks to 'translate' is itself only a ready-formed dictionary, its words only explainable through other words, and so on indefinitely; something experienced in exemplary fashion by the young Thomas de Quincey, he who was so good at Greek that in order to translate absolutely modern ideas and images into that dead language, he had, so Baudelaire tells us (in *Paradis Artificiels*), 'created for himself an unfailing dictionary, vastly more extensive and complex than those resulting from the ordinary patience of purely literary themes'.

Succeeding the Author, the scriptor no longer bears within him passions, humours, feelings, impressions, but rather this immense dictionary from which he draws a writing that can know no halt: life never does more than imitate the book, and the book itself is only a tissue of signs, an imitation that is lost, infinitely deferred.

Once the Author is removed, the claim to decipher a text becomes quite futile. To give a text an Author is to impose a limit on that text, to furnish it with a final signified, to close the writing. Such a conception suits criticism very well, the latter then allotting itself the important task of discovering the Author (or its hypostases: society, history, psyché, liberty) beneath the work: when the Author has been found, the text is 'explained' – victory to the critic. Hence there is no surprise in the fact that, historically, the reign of the Author has also been that of the Critic, nor again in the fact that criticism (be it new) is today undermined along with the Author. In the multiplicity of writing, everything is to be *disentangled*, nothing *deciphered*; the structure can be followed, 'run' (like the thread of a stocking) at every point and at every level, but there is nothing beneath: the space of writing is to be ranged over, not pierced; writing ceaselessly posits meaning ceaselessly to evaporate it, carrying out a systematic exemption of meaning. In precisely this way literature (it would be better from now on to say *writing*), by refusing to assign a 'secret', an ultimate meaning, to the text (and to the world as text), liberates what may be called an anti-theological activity, an activity that is truly revolutionary since to refuse to fix meaning is, in the end, to refuse God and his hypostases – reason, science, law.

Let us come back to the Balzac sentence. No one, no 'person', says it: its source, its voice, is not the true place of the writing, which is reading. Another – very precise –

example will help to make this clear: recent research (J.-P. Vernant[1]) has demonstrated the constitutively ambiguous nature of Greek tragedy, its texts being woven from words with double meanings that each character understands unilaterally (this perpetual misunderstanding is exactly the 'tragic'); there is, however, someone who understands each word in its duplicity and who, in addition, hears the very deafness of the characters speaking in front of him – this someone being precisely the reader (or here, the listener). Thus is revealed the total existence of writing: a text is made of multiple writings, drawn from many cultures and entering into mutual relations of dialogue, parody, contestation, but there is one place where this multiplicity is focused and that place is the reader, not, as was hitherto said, the author. The reader is the space on which all the quotations that make up a writing are inscribed without any of them being lost; a text's unity lies not in its origin but in its destination. Yet this destination cannot any longer be personal: the reader is without history, biography, psychology; he is simply that *someone* who holds together in a single field all the traces by which the written text is constituted. Which is why it is derisory to condemn the new writing in the name of a humanism hypocritically turned champion of the reader's rights. Classic criticism has never paid any attention to the reader; for it, the writer is the only person in literature. We are now beginning to let ourselves be fooled no longer by the arrogant antiphrastical recriminations of good society in favour of the very thing it sets aside, ignores, smothers, or destroys; we know that to give writing its future, it is necessary to overthrow the myth: the birth of the reader must be at the cost of the death of the Author.

1. [Cf. Jean-Pierre Vernant (with Pierre Vidal-Naquet), *Mythe et tragédie en Grèce ancienne*, Paris 1972. esp. pp. 19-40, 99-131.]

Musica Practica

There are two musics (at least so I have always thought): the music one listens to, the music one plays. These two musics are two totally different arts, each with its own history, its own sociology, its own aesthetics, its own erotic; the same composer can be minor if you listen to him, tremendous if you play him (even badly) – such is Schumann.

The music one plays comes from an activity that is very little auditory, being above all manual (and thus in a way much more sensual). It is the music which you or I can play, alone or among friends, with no other audience than its participants (that is, with all risk of theatre, all temptation of hysteria removed); a muscular music in which the part taken by the sense of hearing is one only of ratification, as though the body were hearing – and not 'the soul'; a music which is not played 'by heart': seated at the keyboard or the music stand, the body controls, conducts, co-ordinates, having itself to transcribe what it reads, making sound and meaning, the body as inscriber and not just transmitter, simple receiver. This music has disappeared; initially the province of the idle (aristocratic) class, it lapsed into an insipid social rite with the coming of the democracy of the bourgeoisie (the piano, the young lady, the drawing room, the nocturne) and then faded out altogether (who plays the piano today?). To find practical music in the West, one has now to look to another public, another repertoire, another instrument (the young generation, vocal music, the guitar). Concurrently, passive, receptive music, sound music, is become *the* music (that of concert, festival, record, radio): playing has ceased to exist; musical activity is no longer manual, muscular, kneadingly physical, but merely liquid, effusive, 'lubrificating', to take up a word from Balzac. So too has the performer changed. The amateur, a role defined much more by a style than by a technical imperfection, is no longer anywhere to be found; the professionals, pure specialists whose training remains entirely esoteric for the public (who is there who is still acquainted with the problems of musical education?), never offer that style of the perfect amateur the great value of which could still be recognized in a Lipati or a Panzera, touching off in us not satisfaction but desire, the desire to *make* that music. In short, there was first the actor of music, then the interpreter (the grand Romantic voice), then finally the technician, who relieves the listener of all activity, even by procuration, and abolishes in the sphere of music the very notion of *doing*.

The work of Beethoven seems to me bound up with this historical problem, not as the straightforward expression of a particular moment (the transition from amateur to interpreter) but as the powerful germ of a disturbance of civilization, Beethoven at once bringing together its elements and sketching out its solution; an ambiguity which is that of Beethoven's two historical roles: the mythical role which he was made to play by the whole of the nineteenth century and the modern role which our own century is beginning to accord him (I refer here to Boucourechliev's study[1]).

For the nineteenth century, leaving aside a few stupid representations, such as the one given by Vincent d'Indy who just about makes of Beethoven a kind of reactionary and anti-Semitic hypocrite, Beethoven was the first man of music to be *free*. Now for the first time the fact of having several successive *manners* was held to the glory of an artist; he was acknowledged the right of metamorphosis, he could

1. [A. Boucourechliev, *Beethoven*, Paris 1969.]

be dissatisfied with himself or, more profoundly, with his language, he could change his codes as he went through life (this is what is expressed by Lenz's naive and enthusiastic image of Beethoven's three different manners). From this moment that the work becomes the trace of a movement, of a journey, it appeals to the idea of fate. The artist is in search of his 'truth' and this quest forms an order in itself, a message that can be read, in spite of the variations in its content, over all the work or, at least, whose readability feeds on a sort of totality of the artist: his career, his loves, his ideas, his character, his words become traits of meaning; a Beethovian biography is born (one ought to be able to say a bio-mythology), the artist is brought forward as a complete hero, endowed with a discourse (a rare occurrence for a musician), a legend (a good ten or so anecdotes), an iconography, a race (that of the Titans of Art: Michelangelo, Balzac) and a fatal malady (the deafness of he who creates for the pleasure of our ears). Into this system of meaning that is the Romantic Beethoven are incorporated truly structural features (features which are ambiguous, at once musical and psychological): the paroxysmal development of contrasts in intensity (the signifying opposition of the *piano* and the *forte*, an opposition the historical importance of which is perhaps not very clearly recognized, it characterizing after all only a tiny portion of the music of the world and corresponding to the invention of an instrument whose name is indicative enough, the *piano-forte*), the shattering of the melody, taken as the symbol of restlessness and the seething agitation of creativeness, the emphatic redundancy of moments of excitement and termination (a naive image of fate dealing its blows), the experience of limits (the abolition or the inversion of the traditional parts of musical speech), the production of musical chimera (the voice rising out of the symphony) – and all this, which could easily be transformed metaphorically into pseudo-philosophical values, nonetheless musically acceptable since always deployed under the authority of the fundamental code of the West, tonality.

Further, this romantic image (the meaning of which finally is a certain *discord*) creates a problem of performance: the amateur is unable to master Beethoven's music, not so much by reason of the technical difficulties as by the very breakdown of the code of the former *musica practica*. According to this code, the fantasmatic (that is to say corporal) image which guided the performer was that of a song ('spun out' inwardly); with Beethoven, the mimetic impulse (does not musical fantasy consist in giving oneself a place, as subject, in the scenario of the performance?) becomes orchestral, thus escaping from the fetishism of a single element (voice or rhythm). The body strives to be total, and so the idea of an intimist or familial activity is destroyed: *to want* to play Beethoven is to see oneself as the conductor of an orchestra (the dream of how many children? the tautological dream of how many conductors, a prey in their conducting to all the signs of the panic of possession?). Beethoven's work forsakes the amateur and seems, in an initial moment, to call on the new Romantic deity, the interpreter. Yet here again we are disappointed: who (what soloist, what pianist?) can play Beethoven well? It is as though this music offers only the choice between a 'role' and its absence, the illusion of demiurgy and the prudence of platitude, sublimated as 'renunciation'.

The truth is perhaps that Beethoven's music has in it something *inaudible* (something for which hearing is not the *exact* locality), and this brings us to the second Beethoven. It is not possible that a musician be deaf by pure contingency or poignant destiny (they are the same thing). Beethoven's deafness designates the lack wherein resides all signification; it appeals to a music that is not abstract or inward, but that is endowed, if one may put it like this, with a tangible intelligibility, with the intelligible as tangible. Such a category is truly revolutionary, unthinkable in the terms of the old aesthetics; the work that complies with it cannot be received on the basis of pure sensuality, which is always cultural, nor on that of an intelligible order of (rhetorical, thematic) development, and without it neither the modern text nor contemporary music can be accepted. As we know since Boucourechliev's analyses, this Beethoven is exemplarily the Beethoven of the *Diabelli Variations* and the operation by which we can grasp this Beethoven (and the category he initiates) can no longer be either performance or hearing, but reading. This is not to say that one has to sit with a Beethoven score and get from it an inner recital (which would still remain dependent on the old animistic fantasy); it means that with respect to this music one must put oneself in the position or, better, in the activity of an operator, who knows how to displace, assemble, combine, fit together; in a word (if it is not too worn out), who knows how to structure (very different from constructing or reconstructing in the classic sense). Just as the reading of the modern text (such at least as it may be postulated) consists not in receiving, in knowing or in feeling that text, but in writing it anew, in crossing its writing with a fresh inscription, so too reading this Beethoven is *to operate* his music, to draw it (it is willing to be drawn) into an unknown *praxis*.

In this way may be rediscovered, modified according to the movement of the historical dialectic, a certain *musica practica*. What is the use of composing if it is to confine the product within the precinct of the concert or the solitude of listening to the radio? To compose, at least by propensity, is *to give to do*, not to give to hear but to give to write. The modern location for music is not the concert hall, but the stage on which the musicians pass, in what is often a dazzling display, from one source of sound to another. It is we who are playing, though still it is true by proxy; but one can imagine the concert – later on? – as exclusively a workshop, from which nothing spills over – no dream, no imaginary, in short, no 'soul' and where all the musical art is absorbed in a praxis *with no remainder*. Such is the utopia that a certain Beethoven, who is not played, teaches us to formulate – which is why it is possible now to feel in him a musician with a future.

From Work to Text

It is a fact that over the last few years a certain change has taken place (or is taking place) in our conception of language and, consequently, of the literary work which owes at least its phenomenal existence to this same language. The change is clearly connected with the current development of (amongst other disciplines) linguistics, anthropology, Marxism and psychoanalysis (the term 'connection' is used here in a deliberately neutral way: one does not decide a determination, be it multiple and dialectical). What is new and which affects the idea of the work comes not necessarily from the internal recasting of each of these disciplines, but rather from their encounter in relation to an object which traditionally is the province of none of them. It is indeed as though the *interdisciplinarity* which is today held up as a prime value in research cannot be accomplished by the simple confrontation of specialist branches of knowledge. Interdisciplinarity is not the calm of an easy security; it begins *effectively* (as opposed to the mere expression of a pious wish) when the solidarity of the old disciplines breaks down – perhaps even violently, via the jolts of fashion – in the interests of a new object and a new language neither of which has a place in the field of the sciences that were to be brought peacefully together, this unease in classification being precisely the point from which it is possible to diagnose a certain mutation. The mutation in which the idea of the work seems to be gripped must not, however, be over-estimated: it is more in the nature of an epistemological slide than of a real break. The break, as is frequently stressed, is seen to have taken place in the last century with the appearance of Marxism and Freudianism; since then there has been no further break, so that in a way it can be said that for the last hundred years we have been living in repetition. What History, our History, allows us today is merely to slide, to vary, to exceed, to repudiate. Just as Einsteinian science demands that *the relativity of the frames of reference* be included in the object studied, so the combined action of Marxism, Freudianism and structuralism demands, in literature, the relativization of the relations of writer, reader and observer (critic). Over against the traditional notion of the *work*, for long – and still – conceived of in a, so to speak, Newtonian way, there is now the requirement of a new object, obtained by the sliding or overturning of former categories. That object is the *Text*. I know the word is fashionable (I am myself often led to use it) and therefore regarded by some with suspicion, but that is exactly why I should like to remind myself of the principal propositions at the intersection of which I see the Text as standing. The word 'proposition' is to be understood more in a grammatical than in a logical sense: the following are not argumentations but enunciations, 'touches', approaches that consent to remain metaphorical. Here then are these propositions; they concern method, genres, signs, plurality, filiation, reading and pleasure.

1. The Text is not to be thought of as an object that can be computed. It would be futile to try to separate out materially works from texts. In particular, the tendency must be avoided to say that the work is classic, the text avant-garde; it is not a question of drawing up a crude honours list in the name of modernity and declaring certain literary productions 'in' and others 'out' by virtue of their chronological situation: there may be 'text' in a very ancient work, while many products of contemporary literature are in no way texts. The difference is this: the work is a fragment of substance, occupying a part of the space of

books (in a library for example), the Text is a methodological field. The opposition may recall (without at all reproducing term for term) Lacan's distinction between 'reality' and 'the real': the one is displayed, the other demonstrated; likewise, the work can be seen (in bookshops, in catalogues, in exam syllabuses), the text is a process of demonstration, speaks according to certain rules (or against certain rules); the work can be held in the hand, the text is held in language, only exists in the movement of a discourse (or rather, it is Text for the very reason that it knows itself as text); the Text is not the decomposition of the work, it is the work that is the imaginary tail of the Text; or again, *the Text is experienced only in an activity of production*. It follows that the Text cannot stop (for example on a library shelf); its constitutive movement is that of cutting across (in particular, it can cut across the work, several works).

2. In the same way, the Text does not stop at (good) Literature; it cannot be contained in a hierarchy, even in a simple division of genres. What constitutes the Text is, on the contrary (or precisely), its subversive force in respect of the old classifications. How do you classify a writer like Georges Bataille? Novelist, poet, essayist, economist, philosopher, mystic? The answer is so difficult that the literary manuals generally prefer to forget about Bataille who, in fact, wrote texts, perhaps continuously one single text. If the Text poses problems of classification (which is furthermore one of its 'social' functions), this is because it always involves a certain experience of limits (to take up an expression from Philippe Sollers). Thibaudet used already to talk – but in a very restricted sense – of limit-works (such as Chateaubriand's *Vie de Rancé*, which does indeed come through to us today as a 'text'); the Text is that which goes to the limit of the rules of enunciation (rationality, readability, etc.). Nor is this a rhetorical idea, resorted to for some 'heroic' effect: the Text tries to place itself very exactly

behind the limit of the *doxa* (is not general opinion – constitutive of our democratic societies and powerfully aided by mass communications – defined by its limits, the energy with which it excludes, its *censorship*?). Taking the word literally, it may be said that the Text is always *paradoxical.*

3. The Text can be approached, experienced, in reaction to the sign. The work closes on a signified. There are two modes of signification which can be attributed to this signified: either it is claimed to be evident and the work is then the object of a literal science, of philology, or else it is considered to be secret, ultimate, something to be sought out, and the work then falls under the scope of a hermeneutics, of an interpretation (Marxist, psychoanalytic, thematic, etc.); in short, the work itself functions as a general sign and it is normal that it should represent an institutional category of the civilization of the Sign. The Text, on the contrary, practises the infinite deferment of the signified, is dilatory; its field is that of the signifier and the signifier must not be conceived of as 'the first stage of meaning', its material vestibule, but, in complete opposition to this, as its *deferred action.* Similarly, the *infinity* of the signifier refers not to some idea of the ineffable (the unnameable signified) but to that of a *playing*; the generation of the perpetual signifier (after the fashion of a perpetual calender) in the field of the text (better, of which the text is the field) is realized not according to an organic progress of maturation or a hermeneutic course of deepening investigation, but, rather, according to a serial movement of disconnections, overlappings, variations. The logic regulating the Text is not comprehensive (define 'what the work means') but metonymic; the activity of associations, contiguities, carryings-over coincides with a liberation of symbolic energy (lacking it, man would die); the work – in the best of cases – is *moderately* symbolic (its symbolic runs out, comes to a halt); the Text is *radically* symbolic:

a work conceived, perceived and received in its integrally symbolic nature is a text. Thus is the Text restored to language; like language, it is structured but off-centred, without closure (note, in reply to the contemptuous suspicion of the 'fashionable' sometimes directed at structuralism, that the epistemological privilege currently accorded to language stems precisely from the discovery there of a paradoxical idea of structure: a system with neither close nor centre).

4. The Text is plural. Which is not simply to say that it has several meanings, but that it accomplishes the very plural of meaning: an *irreducible* (and not merely an acceptable) plural. The Text is not a co-existence of meanings but a passage, an overcrossing; thus it answers not to an interpretation, even a liberal one, but to an explosion, a dissemination. The plural of the Text depends, that is, not on the ambiguity of its contents but on what might be called the *stereographic plurality* of its weave of signifiers (etymologically, the text is a tissue, a woven fabric). The reader of the Text may be compared to someone at a loose end (someone slackened off from any imaginary); this passably empty subject strolls – it is what happened to the author of these lines, then it was that he had a vivid idea of the Text – on the side of a valley, a *oued* flowing down below (*oued* is there to bear witness to a certain feeling of unfamiliarity); what he perceives is multiple, irreducible, coming from a disconnected, heterogeneous variety of substances and perspectives: lights, colours, vegetation, heat, air, slender explosions of noises, scant cries of birds, children's voices from over on the other side, passages, gestures, clothes of inhabitants near or far away. All these *incidents* are half-identifiable: they come from codes which are known but their combination is unique, founds the stroll in a difference repeatable only as difference. So the Text: it can be it only in its difference (which does not mean its individuality), its reading is semelfactive (this rendering illusory any

inductive-deductive science of texts – no 'grammar' of the text) and nevertheless woven entirely with citations, references, echoes, cultural languages (what language is not?), antecedent or contemporary, which cut across it through and through in a vast stereophony. The intertextual in which every text is held, it itself being the text-between of another text, is not to be confused with some origin of the text: to try to find the 'sources', the 'influences' of a work, is to fall in with the myth of filiation; the citations which go to make up a text are anonymous, untraceable, and yet *already read*: they are quotations without inverted commas. The work has nothing disturbing for any monistic philosophy (we know that there are opposing examples of these); for such a philosophy, plural is the Evil. Against the work, therefore, the text could well take as its motto the words of the man possessed by demons (*Mark* 5: 9): 'My name is Legion: for we are many.' The plural of demoniacal texture which opposes text to work can bring with it fundamental changes in reading, and precisely in areas where monologism appears to be the Law: certain of the 'texts' of Holy Scripture traditionally recuperated by theological monism (historical or anagogical) will perhaps offer themselves to a diffraction of meanings (finally, that is to say, to a materialist reading), while the Marxist interpretation of works, so far resolutely monistic, will be able to materialize itself more by pluralizing itself (if, however, the Marxist 'institutions' allow it).

5. The work is caught up in a process of filiation. Are postulated: a *determination* of the work by the world (by race, then by History), a *consecution* of works amongst themselves, and a *conformity* of the work to the author. The author is reputed the father and the owner of his work: literary science therefore teaches *respect* for the manuscript and the author's declared intentions, while society asserts the legality of the relation of author to work (the '*droit*

d'auteur' or 'copyright', in fact of recent date since it was only really legalized at the time of the French Revolution). As for the Text, it reads without the inscription of the Father. Here again, the metaphor of the Text separates from that of the work: the latter refers to the image of an *organism* which grows by vital expansion, by 'development' (a word which is significantly ambiguous, at once biological and rhetorical); the metaphor of the Text is that of the *network*; if the Text extends itself, it is as a result of a combinatory systematic (an image, moreover, close to current biological conceptions of the living being). Hence no vital 'respect' is due to the Text: it can be *broken* (which is just what the Middle Ages did with two nevertheless authoritative texts – Holy Scripture and Aristotle); it can be read without the guarantee of its father, the restitution of the inter-text paradoxically abolishing any legacy. It is not that the Author may not 'come back' in the Text, in his text, but he then does so as a 'guest'. If he is a novelist, he is inscribed in the novel like one of his characters, figured in the carpet; no longer privileged, paternal, aletheological, his inscription is ludic. He becomes, as it were, a paper-author: his life is no longer the origin of his fictions but a fiction contributing to his work; there is a reversion of the work on to the life (and no longer the contrary); it is the work of Proust, of Genet which allows their lives to be read as a text. The word 'bio-graphy' re-acquires a strong, etymological sense, at the same time as the sincerity of the enunciation – veritable 'cross' borne by literary morality – becomes a false problem: the *I* which writes the text, it too, is never more than a paper-*I*.

6. The work is normally the object of a consumption; no demagogy is intended here in referring to the so-called consumer culture but it has to be recognized that today it is the 'quality' of the work (which supposes finally an appreciation of 'taste') and not the operation of reading

itself which can differentiate between books: structurally, there is no difference between 'cultured' reading and casual reading in trains. The Text (if only by its frequent 'unreadability') decants the work (the work permitting) from its consumption and gathers it up as play, activity, production, practice. This means that the Text requires that one try to abolish (or at the very least to diminish) the distance between writing and reading, in no way by intensifying the projection of the reader into the work but by joining them in a single signifying practice. The distance separating reading from writing is historical. In the times of the greatest social division (before the setting up of democratic cultures), reading and writing were equally privileges of class. Rhetoric, the great literary code of those times, taught one to *write* (even if what was then normally produced were speeches, not texts). Significantly, the coming of democracy reversed the word of command: what the (secondary) School prides itself on is teaching to *read* (well) and no longer to write (consciousness of the deficiency is becoming fashionable again today: the teacher is called upon to teach pupils to 'express themselves', which is a little like replacing a form of repression by a misconception). In fact, *reading*, in the sense of consuming, is far from *playing* with the text. 'Playing' must be understood here in all its polysemy: the text itself *plays* (like a door, like a machine with 'play') and the reader plays twice over, playing the Text as one plays a game, looking for a practice which re-produces it, but, in order that that practice not be reduced to a passive, inner *mimesis* (the Text is precisely that which resists such a reduction), also playing the Text in the musical sense of the term. The history of music (as a practice, not as an 'art') does indeed parallel that of the Text fairly closely: there was a period when practising amateurs were numerous (at least within the confines of a certain class) and 'playing' and 'listening' formed a scarcely differentiated activity;

then two roles appeared in succession, first that of the performer, the interpreter to whom the bourgeois public (though still itself able to play a little – the whole history of the piano) delegated its playing, then that of the (passive) amateur, who listens to music without being able to play (the gramophone record takes the place of the piano). We know that today post-serial music has radically altered the role of the 'interpreter', who is called on to be in some sort the co-author of the score, completing it rather than giving it 'expression'. The Text is very much a score of this new kind: it asks of the reader a practical collaboration. Which is an important change, for who executes the work? (Mallarmé posed the question, wanting the audience to *produce* the book). Nowadays only the critic executes the work (accepting the play on words). The reduction of reading to a consumption is clearly responsible for the 'boredom' experienced by many in the face of the modern ('unreadable') text, the avant-garde film or painting: to be bored means that one cannot produce the text, open it out, *set it going*.

7. This leads us to pose (to propose) a final approach to the Text, that of pleasure. I do not know whether there has ever been a hedonistic aesthetics (eudæmonist philosophies are themselves rare). Certainly there exists a pleasure of the work (of certain works); I can delight in reading and re-reading Proust, Flaubert, Balzac, even – why not? – Alexandre Dumas. But this pleasure, no matter how keen and even when free from all prejudice, remains in part (unless by some exceptional critical effort) a pleasure of consumption; for if I can read these authors, I also know that I cannot *re-write* them (that it is impossible today to write 'like that') and this knowledge, depressing enough, suffices to cut me off from the production of these works, in the very moment their remoteness establishes my modernity (is not to be modern to know clearly what cannot be

started over again?). As for the Text, it is bound to *jouis sance*, that is to a pleasure without separation. Order of the signifier, the Text participates in its own way in a social utopia; before History (supposing the latter does not opt for barbarism), the Text achieves, if not the transparence of social relations, that at least of language relations: the Text is that space where no language has a hold over any other, where languages circulate (keeping the circular sense of the term).

These few propositions, inevitably, do not constitute the articulations of a Theory of the Text and this is not simply the result of the failings of the person here presenting them (who in many respects has anyway done no more than pick up what is being developed round about him). It stems from the fact that a Theory of the Text cannot be satisfied by a metalinguistic exposition: the destruction of meta-language, or at least (since it may be necessary provisionally to resort to meta-language) its calling into doubt, is part of the theory itself: the discourse on the Text should itself be nothing other than text, research, textual activity, since the Text is that *social* space which leaves no language safe, outside, nor any subject of the enunciation in position as judge, master, analyst, confessor, decoder. The theory of the Text can coincide only with a practice of writing.

Change the Object Itself

Mythology today

Some fifteen years ago now a certain idea of contemporary myth was put forward.[1] That idea, which at its outset was really very little developed, nevertheless contained a number of theoretical articulations:

1. Myth, close to what Durkheimian sociology calls a 'collective representation', can be read in the anonymous utterances of the press, advertising, mass consumer goods; it is something socially determined, a 'reflection'.

2. This reflection, however, in accordance with a famous image used by Marx, is *inverted*: myth consists in overturning culture into nature or, at least, the social, the cultural, the ideological, the historical into the 'natural'. What is nothing but a product of class division and its moral, cultural and aesthetic consequences is presented (stated) as being a 'matter of course'; under the effect of mythical inversion, the quite contingent foundations of the utterance become Common Sense, Right Reason, the Norm, General Opinion, in short the *doxa* (which is the secular figure of the Origin).

3. Contemporary myth is discontinuous. It is no longer expressed in long fixed narratives but only in 'discourse'; at most, it is a *phraseology*, a corpus of phrases (of stereotypes); myth disappears, but leaving – so much the more insidious – the *mythical*.

4. As a type of speech (which was after all the meaning of *muthos*), contemporary myth falls within the province of a semiology; the latter enables the mythical inversion to be

1. R. Barthes, *Mythologies*, Paris 1957 [translated as *Mythologies*, London and New York 1972]; the texts which make up the volume were written between 1954 and 1956.

'righted' by breaking up the message into two semantic systems: a connoted system whose signified is ideological (and thus 'straight', 'non-inverted' or, to be clearer – and accepting a moral language – *cynical*) and a denoted system (the apparent literalness of image, object, sentence) whose function is to naturalize the class proposition by lending it the guarantee of the most 'innocent' of natures, that of language – millennial, maternal, scholastic, etc.

Thus appeared, thus at least appeared to me, myth today. Has anything changed? Not French society, at any rate not at this level, mythical history having a time-scale different to that of political history. Nor the myths, nor even the analysis: in our society the mythical still abounds, just as anonymous and slippery, fragmented and garrulous, available both for ideological criticism and semiological dismantling. No, what has changed these fifteen years is the *science of reading* under whose gaze myth, like an animal long since captured and held in observation, does nevertheless become *a different object*.

A science of the signifier (even if still in process of development), that is, has taken its place in the work of the period and its purpose is less the analysis of the sign than its dislocation. With regard to myth, and though this is a work that is yet to be carried through, the new semiology – or the new mythology – can no longer, will no longer be able to, separate so easily the signifier from the signified, the ideological from the phraseological. It is not that the distinction is false or without its use but rather that it too has become in some sort mythical: any student can and does denounce the bourgeois or petit-bourgeois character of such and such a form (of life, of thought, of consumption). In other words, a mythological doxa has been created: denunciation, demystification (or demythification), has itself become discourse, stock of phrases, catechistic declaration; in the face of which, the science of the signifier can only shift its place and stop (provisionally) further on – no longer at the (analytic) dissociation of the sign but at its very hesitation: it is no longer the myths which need to be unmasked (the doxa now takes care of that), it is the sign itself which must be shaken; the problem is not to reveal the (latent) meaning of an utterance, of a trait, of a narrative, but to fissure the very representation of meaning, is not to change or purify the symbols but to challenge the symbolic itself. In this, (mythological) semiology finds itself a little in the same situation as psychoanalysis before it: the latter began necessarily by drawing up lists of symbols (a tooth falling out is the subject castrated and so on) but its concern today, much more than with such a lexicon (which, without being false, is no longer of interest to it – though of enormous interest to those who dabble in the psychoanalytic vulgate), is with the interrogation of the very dialectic of the signifier; similarly, semiology, which started by establishing a mythological lexicon, is today confronted with a task that is of a more syntactical order (what are the articulations, the displacements, which make up the mythological tissue of a mass consumer society?). In an initial moment, the aim was the destruction of the (ideological) signified; in a second, it is that of the destruction of the sign: 'mythoclasm' is succeeded by a 'semioclasm' which is much more far-reaching and pitched at a different level. The historical field of action is thus widened: no longer the (narrow) sphere of French society but far beyond that, historically and geographically, the whole of Western civilization (Graeco-Judaeo-Islamo-Christian), unified under the one theology (Essence, monotheism) and identified by the regime of meaning it practices – from Plato to *France-Dimanche*.

The science of the signifier brings contemporary mythology a second rectification (or a second enlargement). Taken aslant by language, the world is written through and through; signs, endlessly deferring their foundations, transforming their signifieds into new signifiers, infinitely citing one another, nowhere come to a halt: writing is generalized. If the alienation of society still demands the demystification of languages (and notably the language of myths), the direction this combat must take is not, is no longer, that of critical decipherment but that of *evaluation*. Faced with all the writings of the world, with the skein of different forms of discourse (didactic, aesthetic, informative, political, etc.), it is a question of estimating levels of reification, degrees of phraseological density. Will we be able to render precise a notion which seems to me essential, that of the *compactness* of a language? Languages are more or less *thick*; certain amongst them, the most social, the most mythical, present an unshakeable homogeneity (there is a real force of meaning, a war of meanings): woven with habits and repetitions, with stereotypes, obligatory final clauses and key-words, each constitutes an *idiolect*, or more exactly a *sociolect* (a notion to which twenty years ago I gave the name of *writing*[1]). Thus, rather than myths, it is sociolects which must today be distinguished and described; which means that mythologies would be succeeded by an idiolectology – more formal and thereby, I believe, more penetrating – whose operational concepts would no longer be sign, signifier, signified and connotation but citation, reference, stereotype. In this way, thick languages (such as the discourse of myth) could be taken up in the line of a trans-writing of which the text (that we still refer to as 'literary'), the antidote of myth, would be the extreme pole or rather the region – airy, light, spaced, open, uncentred, noble and free – where writing spreads itself against the idiolect, at its limit and fighting it. Myth, indeed, must be included in a general theory of language, of writing, of the signifier, and this theory, resting on the formulations of

1. [R. Barthes, *Le Degré zéro de l'écriture*, Paris 1953; translated as *Writing Degree Zero*, London 1967 and New York 1968.]

ethnology, psychoanalysis, semiology and ideological analysis must widen its object so as to take in the *sentence* or, better, to take in *sentences* (the plural of the sentence). What I mean by this is that the mythical is present everywhere *sentences are turned*, *stories told* (in all senses of the two expressions): from inner speech to conversation, from newspaper article to political sermon, from novel (if there still are any) to advertising image – all utterances which could be brought together under the Lacanian concept of the *imaginary*.

This is no more than a programme, perhaps only an 'inclination'. I believe, however, that even if the new semiology – concerned in particular recently with the literary text – has not applied itself further to the myths of our time since the last of the texts in *Mythologies* where I sketched out an initial semiotic approach to social language, it is at least conscious of its task: no longer simply to *upend* (or *right*) the mythical message, to stand it back on its feet, with denotation at the bottom and connotation at the top, nature on the surface and class interest deep down, but rather to change the object itself, to produce a new object, point of departure for a new science, to move – with all due allowance for difference in importance (obviously) and according to Althusser's scheme – from Feuerbach to Marx, from the young Marx to the mature Marx.

Lesson in Writing

The puppets of Bunraku theatre are from three to five feet in height. They are little men or women with movable limbs, hands and mouth. Each puppet is worked by three men who remain in view, surrounding, supporting and accompanying it. The principal operator controls the upper part of the doll and its right arm; his face is visible, smooth, clear, impassive, cold like 'a white onion freshly washed'[1]. The two assistants are clad in black, their faces hidden by a piece of cloth; the first, gloved but with thumb exposed, holds a large scissors mechanism with which he operates the doll's left arm and hand; the second, crawling along on his knees, supports the body, makes it walk. These men move about along a low trench which leaves them unconcealed. The scenery is behind them, as at the theatre. To the side, there is a dais for the musicians and the narrators whose role is to *express* the text (a little as one presses out the juice of a fruit); this text is half-spoken, half-sung and, punctuated with great plectrum strokes by the samisen players, is at once measured and thrown off, given with violence and artifice. Sweating and motionless, the mouthpieces sit behind little lecterns on which rests the writing they must vocalize, its vertical characters glimpsed from afar when they turn a page of their libretto; a triangle of stiff canvas fixed to their shoulders like a kite frames their faces, faces in throes to all the torments of the voice.

1. Haiku by Bashô:
   A white onion
   freshly washed.
   Feeling of cold.

Antithesis is a privileged figure of our culture, doubtless because it corresponds well to our vision of good and evil and to that inveterate emblematism which has us turn every word into a watchword against its opposite (creativity versus intelligence, spontaneity versus reflection, truth versus appearance, etc.). Bunraku cares nothing for these contraries, for this antonymy that regulates our whole morality of discourse; concerned with a fundamental antilogy, that of the *animate/inanimate*, it disturbs it, dissipates it to the advantage of neither of the terms. With us, the marionette (Punch for example) is there to hold up to the actor the mirror of his opposite, animating the in-animate but so as the better to reveal its degradation, the abjectness of its inertia; a caricature of 'life', it affirms precisely thereby life's *moral* limits and serves to confine beauty, truth and emotion in the living body of the actor – he who nevertheless makes of that body a lie. Bunraku on the other hand does not ape the actor, it rids us of him. How? Exactly by a certain reflection on the human body here conducted by inanimate matter with infinitely more rigour and excitement than by the animate body (endowed with a 'soul'). The (naturalistic) Western actor is never beautiful, his body is intended as essentially physiological and not plastic; it is a collection of organs, a musculature of passions, whose every resource (voice, facial expressions, gestures) is subject to a kind of gymnastic drill. By a reversal that is specifically bourgeois, the actor's body, although built on a division of the essences of passion, then borrows from physiology the alibi of an organic unity, the unity of 'life'. In this way it is the actor who is a marionette and this despite the smooth flow of his acting, the model for which is not the caress but only the visceral 'truth'.

Thus, beneath a 'living' and 'natural' outward appearance, the Western actor maintains the division of his body and, consequently, the food of our fantasies. Voice, look, figure are in turn eroticized, like so many pieces of the body, like so many fetishes. The Western marionette too (as is evident in Punch) is a by-product of fantasy: as reduction, a grating reflection with an adherence to the human order ceaselessly recalled by a caricatural simulation, it lives not as a total body, totally vibrating, but as a rigid portion of the actor of whom it is an emanation; as automaton, it is again a fragment of movement, a start, a jolt, essence of discontinuity, fractured projection of bodily gestures; as doll finally, a reminiscence of the bit of material, of the genital swathe, it is indeed the phallic 'little thing' (*das Kleine*), fallen from the body to become a fetish.

It may well be that the Japanese marionette retains something of this fantasy origin; the art of Bunraku, however, endows it with a different meaning. Bunraku does not aim at 'animating' an inanimate object in such a way as to bring to life a piece of the body, a scrap of man, while preserving its vocation as 'part'; it is not the simulation of the body that it is after, but, as it were, its concrete abstraction. Everything which we attribute to the total body and which is refused to our actors under pretence of a 'living' organic unity is taken up and stated without any falsehood by the Bunraku puppet: fragility, discretion, sumptuousness, extraordinary nuance, abandonment of all triviality, melodic phrasing of gestures, in short those very qualities that the dreams of the old theology granted to the glorified body, namely impassiveness, clarity, agility, subtlety. This is what Bunraku accomplishes, this is how it converts the body-fetish into a lovable body, this is how it refuses the antinomy of *animate/inanimate* and dismisses the concept hiding behind all *animation* of matter, that, quite simply, of 'the soul'.

Another opposition destroyed is that of *inner/outer*. Consider the Western theatre of the last few centuries. Its function is essentially to reveal what is reputed to be secret ('feelings', 'situations', 'conflicts') while concealing the very artifice of the process of revelation (machinery, painting, make-up, sources of light). The Italian stage is the space of this deceit, everything there taking place in a room surreptitiously thrown open, surprised, spied on and relished by a hidden spectator; a theological space, that of the moral falling: on the one side, under a light of which he pretends to be unaware, the actor, that is to say, gesture and speech; on the other, in the darkness, the public, that is to say, consciousness and conscience. Bunraku does not directly subvert the relation between stage and auditorium (any more than did Brecht), though Japanese theatres are infinitely less confined, less suffocating, less ponderous than ours. What it changes, more profoundly, is the driving link between character and actor which is always conceived by us as the expressive channel of an interiority. It has to be remembered that the agents of the spectacle in Bunraku are both visible and impassive. The men in black busy themselves around the doll but without any affectation of skill or discretion, without any promotional demagogy: silent, rapid, elegant, their actions are eminently transitive, operational, coloured by that mixture of strength and subtlety that characterizes Japanese gestuality and that can be seen as the aesthetic envelope of efficacy. As for the master, it has already been said that his head is left uncovered, smooth and bare, without make-up, this conferring on him a *civic* (and not a theatrical) appearance; his face is offered to the spectator for reading, but what is so carefully and so preciously given to be read is that there is nothing to be read – here we find that exemption from meaning which does indeed illumine so many works of the East and which we are scarcely able to comprehend, since for us to attack meaning is to conceal or oppose it, never to absent it. With Bunraku, the sources of the theatre are exposed in their void. What is expelled from the stage is hysteria, that is theatre itself, and what is put in its place is the action necessary for the production of the spectacle – work is substituted for interiority.

It is thus futile to ask oneself as do certain Europeans (Claudel among them) whether or not the spectator can forget the presence of the manipulators. Bunraku practises neither the dissimulation nor the emphatic disclosure of its various mechanisms, hence ridding the animation of the actor of any suggesiton of the sacred and abolishing the metaphysical bond that the West cannot stop itself from setting up between soul and body, cause and effect, motor and machine, agent and actor, Fate and man, God and creature:[1] if the manipulator is not hidden, then why and how turn him into a God? In Bunraku, the puppet is held by no thread; without a thread, there is no longer any metaphor, any Fate; puppet no longer aping creature, man is no longer a puppet in the hands of the deity, the *inner* no longer controls the *outer*.

Finally, a still more radical undertaking, Bunraku attacks the writing of the spectacle. With us, such writing involves an illusion of totality. 'We find nothing more difficult,' says Brecht, 'than to break with the habit of considering an artistic production *as a whole*.'[2] No doubt it is for this reason that periodically, from the Greek *choréia* to the bourgeois opera, we conceive of lyric art as the simultaneity of several modes of expression (acted, sung, mimed) with a sole, indivisible, origin. This origin is the body and the required totality has for its model organic

1. 'Bunraku . . . is, quite simply, metaphysical theatre . . . The puppet is man. The manipulator is God. The assistants are the messengers of Fate.' J.-L. Barrault, 'Le Bunraku', in *Cahiers Renaud-Barrault* 31, November 1960, p. 53.

2. Bertolt Brecht, 'Effets d'éloignement dans l'art du comédien chinois', *Ecrits sur le théâtre* I, Paris 1963, p. 121 ['Alienation effects in Chinese acting', *Brecht on Theatre*, London 1973, p. 91 – with somewhat different wording].

unity. Western spectacle is anthropomorphous:[1] gesture and speech (not to mention song) form but a single tissue, conglomerate and lubrificated like a unique muscle that sets expression going without ever dividing it: the unity of movement and voice produces *the one* who acts; in other words, it is in this unity that is constituted the person of the personage, that is, the actor. In Bunraku, however, no one is on stage, or, more precisely, no person has taken up position there. The (personal) corporal illusion disappears, not because the actors are made of wood and cloth (we saw that Bunraku designates on the contrary a certain *lovableness* of the human body) but because the codes of expression are detached from one another, pulled free from the sticky organicism in which they are held by Western theatre.

In fact then, Bunraku practises three separate writings which are given for reading simultaneously in three areas of the spectacle: the marionette, the manipulator, the vociferator; the effected gesture, the effective gesture, the vocal gesture. The voice is what is really at stake in modernity, the voice as specific substance of language everywhere triumphantly pushed forward. Modern society (as has been repeated often enough) believes itself to be ushering in a civilization of the image, but what it actually establishes overall, and particularly in its leisure activities which are massively spoken, is a civilization of speech. In complete contrast, Bunraku has a *limited* conception of the voice; not suppressing it, it assigns it a clearly defined function that is essentially trivial. The narrator's voice gathers together extravagant declamation, tremulous quiver, shrill feminine tones, broken intonations, tears, paroxysms of anger and lamentation, supplication and astonishment, indecent pathos, the whole concoction of emotion openly prepared at the level of this visceral, inner body of which the larynx

1. Aristotle: 'The action . . . being one and whole like a living being' *Poetics* 1459a.

is the mediating muscle. Even then, such excess is only presented in terms of the very code of the excessive: the voice moves only through a few discontinuous signs of fury; expelled from a body that remains motionless, mounted in the triangle of the costume, linked to the book which guides it from the lectern, studded sharply by the slightly off-phased (and so non-pertinent) strokes of the samisen player, the vocal substance stays written, discontinued, obedient to an irony (if one accepts the word free from any sense of a caustic humour). Thus what the voice exteriorizes finally is not what it carries in it ('feelings') but itself, its own prostitution; while pretending to deliver over contents (anecdotes, passions), the signifier artfully does nothing but turn itself inside out, like a glove.

Hence the voice, without being eliminated (which would be a way of censuring it, that is, of indicating its importance), is set aside (theatrically, the narrators occupy a lateral dais). Bunraku gives the voice a counterbalance, or better a countermarch, that of gesture. Gesture here is twofold: emotive gesture with the marionette (people cry at the suicide of the doll-lover); transitive action with the manipulators. In our theatrical art the actor pretends to engage in action but his actions are never anything but gestures: on stage, nothing but theatre, and yet a theatre that is ashamed. Bunraku (this is its definition) separates the act from the gesture: it exhibits the gesture, it allows the act to be seen; it exposes at once the art and the work, keeping for each its own particular writing. The voice (and there is then no risk in letting it run the gamut of its excesses) is folded into an immense volume of silence in which other traits, other writings, are inscribed with so much finesse. It is here that an extraordinary effect occurs: far from the voice and almost without mimicry, these silent writings – the one transitive, the other gestural – produce an exaltation as special, perhaps, as the intellectual hyperaesthesia attributed to certain drugs. Speech being not purified (Bunraku knows no ascetic ambition) but, as it were, *massed* on the side, the tackily clinging substances of Western theatre are dissolved: emotion no longer submerges everything in its flood but becomes matter for reading; the stereotypes disappear without however the spectacle falling into originality, the 'stroke of genius'. All of which has an evident kinship with the distancing effect recommended by Brecht who was, as perhaps needs recalling, the first to understand and state the critical importance of oriental theatre. This distance, reputed by us to be impossible, useless or derisory and speedily abandoned, despite its being placed by Brecht very precisely at the centre of revolutionary dramatic art (the latter doubtless explains the former), is what Bunraku shows – shows how it can function: by the discontinuity of codes, by the cæsura imposed in the different traits of the representation, so that the *copy* elaborated on the stage is not destroyed but shattered, scored, freed from the metonymical contagion of voice and gesture, soul and body, which entangles our actors.

A total spectacle, but divided, Bunraku evidently excludes improvization, doubtless aware that the return to spontaneity is the return to all those stereotypes which go to make up our 'inner depths'. Here we have, as Brecht saw in connection with the oriental actor whose lesson he wished to receive and propagate on this point too, the reign of the *quotation*,[1] the pinch of writing, the fragment of code, none of the promoters of the action being able to take

1. 'He limits himself from the start to simply quoting the character played. But with what art he does this! He only needs a minimum of illusion. What he has to show is worth seeing even for a man in his right mind.' Brecht, ibid., p. 121 [trans. p. 94]; and elsewhere: 'Once the idea of total transformation is given up, the actor speaks his part not as if he were improvising it himself but like a quotation.' 'Nouvelle technique d'interprétation', ibid., p. 150 ['New techniques of acting', trans. p. 138].

responsibility in his own person for what he is never alone in writing. As in the modern text, the tressing of codes, references, discontinuous observations, anthological gestures, multiplies the written line, and this not by virtue of some metaphysical appeal but by the play of a combinatory set which opens in the entire space of the theatre: what is started by the one is continued by the other, unendingly.

The Grain of the Voice

Language, according to Benveniste, is the only semiotic system capable of *interpreting* another semiotic system (though undoubtedly there exist limit works in the course of which a system feigns self-interpretation – *The Art of the Fugue*). How, then, does language manage when it has to interpret music? Alas, it seems, very badly. If one looks at the normal practice of music criticism (or, which is often the same thing, of conversations 'on' music), it can readily be seen that a work (or its performance) is only ever translated into the poorest of linguistic categories: the adjective. Music, by natural bent, is that which at once receives an adjective. The adjective is inevitable: this music is *this*, this execution is *that*. No doubt the moment we turn an art into a subject (for an article, for a conversation) there is nothing left but to give it predicates; in the case of music, however, such predication unfailingly takes the most facile and trivial form, that of the epithet. Naturally, this epithet, to which we are constantly led by weakness or fascination (little parlour game: talk about a piece of music without using a single adjective), has an economic function: the predicate is always the bulwark with which the subject's imaginary protects itself from the loss which threatens it. The man who provides himself or is provided with an adjective is now hurt, now pleased, but always *constituted*. There is an imaginary in music whose function is to re-assure, to constitute the subject hearing it (would it be that music is dangerous – the old Platonic idea? that music is an access to *jouissance*, to loss, as numerous ethnographic and popular examples would tend to show?) and this imaginary immediately comes to language via the adjective. A historical dossier ought to be assembled here, for adjectival criticism (or predicative interpretation) has taken on over the centuries certain institutional aspects. The musical adjective becomes legal whenever an *ethos* of music is postulated, each time, that is, that music is attributed a regular – natural or magical – mode of signification. Thus with the ancient Greeks, for whom it was the musical *language* (and not the contingent work) in its denotative structure which was immediately adjectival, each mode being linked to a coded expression (rude, austere, proud, virile, solemn, majestic, warlike, educative, noble, sumptuous, doleful, modest, dissolute, voluptuous); thus with the Romantics, from Schumann to Debussy, who substitute for, or add to, the simple indication of tempo (*allegro*, *presto*, *andante*) poetic, emotive predicates which are increasingly refined and which are given in the national language so as to diminish the mark of the code and develop the 'free' character of the predication (*sehr kräftig*, *sehr präcis*, *spirituel et discret*, etc.).

Are we condemned to the adjective? Are we reduced to the dilemma of either the predicable or the ineffable? To ascertain whether there are (verbal) means for talking about music without adjectives, it would be necessary to look at more or less the whole of music criticism, something which I believe has never been done and which, nevertheless, I have neither the intention nor the means of doing here. This much, however, can be said: it is not by struggling against the adjective (diverting the adjective you find on the tip of the tongue towards some substantive or verbal periphrasis) that one stands a chance of exorcising music commentary and liberating it from the fatality of predication; rather than trying to change directly the language on music, it would be better to change the musical object itself, as it presents itself to discourse, better to alter its level of perception or intellection, to displace the fringe of contact between music and language.

It is this displacement that I want to outline, not with regard to the whole of music but simply to a part of vocal music (*lied* or *mélodie*): the very precise space (genre) of *the encounter between a language and a voice*. I shall straightaway give a name to this signifier at the level of which, I believe, the temptation of ethos can be liquidated (and thus the adjective banished): the *grain*, the grain of the voice when the latter is in a dual posture, a dual production – of language and of music.

What I shall attempt to say of the 'grain' will, of course, be only the apparently abstract side, the impossible account of an individual thrill that I constantly experience in listening to singing. In order to disengage this 'grain' from the acknowledged values of vocal music, I shall use a twofold opposition: theoretical, between the pheno-text and the geno-text (borrowing from Julia Kristeva), and paradigmatic, between two singers, one of whom I like very much (although he is no longer heard), the other very little (although one hears no one but him), Panzera and Fischer-Dieskau (here merely ciphers: I am not deifying the first nor attacking the second).

Listen to a Russian bass (a church bass – opera is a genre in which the voice has gone over in its entirety to dramatic expressivity, a voice with a grain which little signifies): something is there, manifest and stubborn (one hears only *that*), beyond (or before) the meaning of the words, their form (the litany), the melisma, and even the style of execution: something which is directly the cantor's body, brought to your ears in one and the same movement from deep down in the cavities, the muscles, the membranes, the cartilages, and from deep down in the Slavonic language, as though a single skin lined the inner flesh of the performer and the music he sings. The voice is not personal: it expresses nothing of the cantor, of his soul; it is not original (all Russian cantors have roughly the same voice), and at the same time it is individual: it has us hear a body which has no civil identity, no 'personality', but which is nevertheless a separate body. Above all, this voice bears along *directly* the symbolic, over the intelligible, the expressive: here, thrown in front of us like a packet, is the Father, his phallic stature. The 'grain' is that: the materiality of the body speaking its mother tongue; perhaps the letter, almost certainly *signifiance*.

Thus we can see in song (pending the extension of this distinction to the whole of music) the two texts described by Julia Kristeva. The *pheno-song* (if the transposition be allowed) covers all the phenomena, all the features which belong to the structure of the language being sung, the rules of the genre, the coded form of the melisma, the composer's idiolect, the style of the interpretation: in short, everything in the performance which is in the service of communication, representation, expression, everything which it is customary to talk about, which forms the tissue of cultural values (the matter of acknowledged tastes, of fashions, of critical commentaries), which takes its bearing directly on the ideological alibis of a period ('subjectivity', 'expressivity', 'dramaticism', 'personality' of the artist). The *geno-song* is the volume of the singing and speaking voice, the space where significations germinate 'from within language and in its very materiality'; it forms a signifying play having nothing to do with communication, representation (of feelings), expression; it is that apex (or that depth) of production where the melody really works at the language – not at what it says, but the voluptuousness of its sounds-signifiers, of its letters – where melody explores how the language works and identifies with that work. It is, in a very simple word but which must be taken seriously, the *diction* of the language.

From the point of view of the pheno-song, Fischer-Dieskau is assuredly an artist beyond reproach: everything in the (semantic and lyrical) structure is respected and yet nothing seduces, nothing sways us to *jouissance*. His art is inordinately expressive (the diction is dramatic, the pauses, the checkings and releasings of breath, occur like shudders of passion) and hence never exceeds culture: here it is the soul which accompanies the song, not the body. What is difficult is for the body to accompany the musical diction not with a movement of emotion but with a 'gesture-support';[1] all the more so since the whole of musical pedagogy teaches not the culture of the 'grain' of the voice but the emotive modes of its delivery – the myth of respiration. How many singing teachers have we not heard prophesying that the art of vocal music rested entirely on the mastery, the correct discipline of breathing! The breath is the *pneuma*, the soul swelling or breaking, and any exclusive art of breathing is likely to be a secretly mystical art (a mysticism levelled down to the measure of the long-playing record). The lung, a stupid organ (lights for cats!), swells but gets no erection; it is in the throat, place where the phonic metal hardens and is segmented, in the mask that *signifiance* explodes, bringing not the soul but *jouissance*. With FD, I seem only to hear the lungs, never the tongue, the glottis, the teeth, the mucous membranes, the nose. All of Panzera's art, on the contrary, was in the letters, not in the bellows (simple technical feature: you never heard him *breathe* but only divide up the phrase). An extreme rigour of thought regulated the prosody of the enunciation and the phonic economy of the French language; prejudices

1. 'Which is why the best way to read me is to accompany the reading with certain appropriate bodily movements. Against non-spoken writing, against non-written speech. For the gesture-support.' Philippe Sollers, *Lois*, Paris 1972, p. 108.

(generally stemming from oratorical and ecclesiastical diction) were overthrown. With regard to the consonants, too readily thought to constitute the very armature of our language (which is not, however, a Semitic one) and always prescribed as needing to be 'articulated', detached, emphasized *in order to fulfil the clarity of meaning*, Panzera recommended that in many cases they be *patinated*, given the wear of a language that had been living, functioning, and working for ages past, that they be made simply the springboard for the admirable vowels. There lay the 'truth' of language – not its functionality (clarity, expressivity, communication) – and the range of vowels received all the *signifiance* (which is meaning in its potential voluptuousness): the opposition of *é* and *è* (so necessary in conjugation), the purity – almost *electronic*, so much was its sound tightened, raised, exposed, held – of the most French of vowels, the *ü* (a vowel not derived by French from Latin). Similarly, Panzera carried his *r*'s beyond the norms of the singer – without denying those norms. His *r* was of course rolled, as in every classic art of singing, but the roll had nothing peasant-like or Canadian about it; it was an artificial roll, the paradoxical state of a letter-sound at once totally abstract (by its metallic brevity of vibration) and totally material (by its manifest deep-rootedness in the action of the throat). This phonetics – am I alone in perceiving it? am I hearing voices within the voice? but isn't it the truth of the voice to be hallucinated? isn't the entire space of the voice an infinite one? which was doubtless the meaning of Saussure's work on anagrams – does not exhaust *signifiance* (which is inexhaustible) but it does at least hold in check the attempts at *expressive reduction* operated by a whole culture against the poem and its melody.

It would not be too difficult to date that culture, to define it historically. FD now reigns more or less unchallenged over the recording of vocal music; he has recorded everything. If you like Schubert but not FD, then Schubert is today *forbidden* you – an example of that positive censorship (censorship by repletion) which characterizes mass culture though it is never criticized. His art – expressive, dramatic, *sentimentally clear*, borne by a voice lacking in any 'grain', in signifying weight, fits well with the demands of an *average* culture. Such a culture, defined by the growth of the number of listeners and the disappearance of practitioners (no more amateurs), wants art, wants music, provided they be clear, that they 'translate' an emotion and represent a signified (the 'meaning' of a poem); an art that innoculates pleasure (by reducing it to a known, coded emotion) and reconciles the subject to what in music *can be said*: what is said about it, predicatively, by Institution, Criticism, Opinion. Panzera does not belong to this culture (he could not have done, having sung before the coming of the microgroove record; moreover I doubt whether, were he singing today, his art would be recognized or even simply *perceived*); his reign, very great between the wars, was that of an exclusively bourgeois art (an art, that is, in no way petit-bourgeois) nearing the end of its inner development and, by a familiar distortion, separated from History. It is perhaps, precisely and less paradoxically than it seems, because this art was *already* marginal, mandarin, that it was able to bear traces of *signifiance*, to escape the tyranny of meaning.

The 'grain' of the voice is not – or is not merely – its timbre; the *signifiance* it opens cannot better be defined, indeed, than by the very friction between the music and something else, which something else is the particular language (and nowise the message). The song must speak, must *write* – for what is produced at the level of the geno-song is finally writing. This sung writing of language is, as I see it, what the French *mélodie* sometimes tried to accomplish. I am well aware that the German *lied* was intimately bound up with the German language via the Romantic poem, that the poetical culture of Schumann was immense and that this same Schumann used to say of Schubert that had he lived into old age he would have set the whole of German literature to music, but I think nevertheless that the historical meaning of the *lied* must be sought in the music (if only because of its popular origins). By contrast, the historical meaning of the *mélodie* is a certain culture of the French language. As we know, the Romantic poetry of France is more oratorical than textual; what the poetry could not accomplish on its own, however, the *mélodie* has occasionally accomplished with it, working at the language through the poem. Such a work (in the specificity here acknowledged it) is not to be seen in the general run of the *mélodies* produced which are too accommodating towards minor poets, the model of the petit-bourgeois romance, and salon usages, but in some few pieces it is indisputable – anthologically (a little by chance) in certain songs by Fauré and Duparc, massively in the later (prosodic) Fauré and the vocal work of Debussy (even if *Pelléas* is often sung badly – dramatically). What is engaged in these works is, much more than a musical style, a practical reflection (if one may put it like that) on the language; there is a progressive movement from the language to the poem, from the poem to the song and from the song to its performance. Which means that the *mélodie* has little to do with the history of music and much with the theory of the text. Here again, the signifier must be redistributed.

Compare two sung deaths, both of them famous: that of Boris and that of Mélisande. Whatever Mussorgsky's intentions, the death of Boris is *expressive* or, if preferred, *hysterical*; it is overloaded with historical, affective contents. Performances of the death cannot be but dramatic: it is the triumph of the pheno-text, the smothering of *signifiance* under the soul as signified. Mélisande, on the contrary, only dies *prosodically*. Two extremes are joined, woven together: the perfect intelligibility of the denotation and the pure prosodic segmentation of the enunciation; between the two a salutary gap (filled out in Boris) – the *pathos*, that is to say, according to Aristotle (why not?), passion *such as men speak and imagine it*, the accepted idea of death, *endoxical* death. Mélisande dies *without any noise* (understanding the term in its cybernetic sense): nothing occurs to interfere with the signifier and there is thus no compulsion to redundance; simply, the production of a music-language with the function of preventing the singer from being expressive. As with the Russian bass, the symbolic (the death) is thrown immediately (without mediation) before us (this to forestall the stock idea which has it that what is not expressive can only be cold and intellectual; Mélisande's death is 'moving', which means that it shifts something in the chain of the signifier).

The *mélodie* disappeared – sank to the bottom – for a good many reasons, or at least the disappearance took on a good many aspects. Doubtless it succumbed to its salon image, this being a little the ridiculous form of its class origin. Mass 'good' music (records, radio) has left it behind, preferring either the more pathetic orchestra (success of Mahler) or less bourgeois instruments than the piano (harpsichord, trumpet). Above all, however, the death of the *mélodie* goes along with a much wider historical phenomenon to a large extent unconnected to the history of music or of musical taste: the French are abandoning their language, not, assuredly, as a normative set of noble values (clarity, elegance, correctness) – or at least this does not bother me very much for these are institutional values – but as a space of pleasure, of thrill, a site where language works *for nothing*, that is, in perversion (remember here the singularity – the solitude – of *Lois* by Philippe Sollers, theatre of the return of the prosodic and metrical work of the language).

The 'grain' is the body in the voice as it sings, the hand as it writes, the limb as it performs. If I perceive the 'grain' in a piece of music and accord this 'grain' a theoretical value (the emergence of the text in the work), I inevitably set up a new scheme of evaluation which will certainly be individual – I am determined to listen to my relation with the body of the man or woman singing or playing and that relation is erotic – but in no way 'subjective' (it is not the psychological 'subject' in me who is listening; the climactic pleasure hoped for is not going to reinforce – to express – that subject but, on the contrary, to lose it). The evaluation will be made outside of any law, outplaying not only the law of culture but equally that of anticulture, developing beyond the subject all the value hidden behind 'I like' or 'I don't like'. Singers especially will be ranged in what may be called, since it is a matter of my choosing without there being any reciprocal choice of me, two prostitutional categories. Thus I shall freely extol such and such a performer, little-known, minor, forgotten, dead perhaps, and turn away from such another, an acknowledged star (let us refrain from examples, no doubt of merely biographical significance); I shall extend my choice across all the genres of vocal music including popular music, where I shall have no difficulty in rediscovering the distinction between the pheno-song and the geno-song (some popular singers have a 'grain' while others, however famous, do not). What is more, leaving aside the voice, the 'grain' – or the lack of it – persists in instrumental music; if the latter no longer has language to lay open *signifiance* in all its volume, at least there is the performer's body which again forces me to evaluation. I shall not judge a performance according to the rules of interpretation, the constraints of style (anyway highly illusory), which almost all belong to the pheno-song (I shall not wax lyrical concerning the 'rigour', the 'brilliance', the 'warmth', the 'respect for what is written', etc.), but according to the image of the body (the figure) given me. I can hear with certainty – the certainty of the body, of thrill – that the harpsichord playing of Wanda Landowska comes from her inner body and not from the petty digital scramble of so many harpsichordists (so much so that it is a different instrument). As for piano music, I know at once which part of the body is playing – if it is the arm, too often, alas, muscled like a dancer's calves, the clutch of the finger-tips (despite the sweeping flourishes of the wrists), or if on the contrary it is the only erotic part of a pianist's body, the pad of the fingers whose 'grain' is so rarely heard (it is hardly necessary to recall that today, under the pressure of the mass long-playing record, there seems to be a flattening out of technique; which is paradoxical in that the various manners of playing are all flattened out *into perfection*: nothing is left but pheno-text).

This discussion has been limited to 'classical music'. It goes without saying, however, that the simple consideration of 'grain' in music could lead to a different history of music from the one we know now (which is purely pheno-textual). Were we to succeed in refining a certain 'aesthetics' of musical pleasure, then doubtless we would attach less importance to the formidable break in tonality accomplished by modernity.

Writers, Intellectuals, Teachers

What follows depends on the idea that there is a fundamental tie between teaching and speech. The idea is a very old one (did not the whole of our teaching spring from Rhetoric?) but it is possible today to consider it differently from yesterday: firstly, because there is a (political) crisis in teaching; secondly, because (Lacanian) psychoanalysis has shown the mechanism of the twists and turns of empty speech; lastly, because the opposition between speech and writing has become an obvious fact with effects that now need to be gradually drawn out.

Over against the teacher, who is on the side of speech, let us call a *writer* every operator of language on the side of writing; between the two, the intellectual, the person who prints and publishes his speech. Between the language of the teacher and that of the intellectual there is hardly any incompatibility (they often co-exist in a single individual); but the writer stands apart, separate. Writing begins at the point where speech becomes *impossible* (a word that can be understood in the sense it has when applied to a child).

Two constraints

Speech is irreversible: a word cannot be *retracted*, except precisely by saying that one retracts it. To cross out is here to add: if I want to erase what I have just said, I cannot do it without showing the eraser itself (I must say: '*or rather ...*' '*I expressed myself badly ...*'); paradoxically, it is ephemeral speech which is indelible, not monumental writing. All that one can do in the case of a spoken utterance is to tack on another utterance. The correcting and improving movement of speech is the wavering of a flow of words, a weave which wears itself out catching itself up, a chain of augmentative corrections which constitutes the favoured abode of the unconscious part of our discourse (it is not by chance that psychoanalysis is linked to speech and not writing: dreams are spoken not written). The eponymous figure of the speaker is Penelope.

Nor is this all. We can only make ourselves understood (well or poorly) if we maintain a certain speed of delivery. We are like a cyclist or a film obliged to keep going so as to avoid falling or scratching. Silence and vacillation are equally forbidden: the articulatory speed binds each point of the sentence to what immediately follows or precedes (impossible to have the word 'set off' towards distant and strange paradigms). Context is a structural given not of language but of speech and it is the very status of context to be reductive of meaning. The spoken word is 'clear'; the banishment of polysemy (such banishment being the definition of 'clarity') serves the Law – *all speech is on the side of the Law*.

Whoever · prepares to speak (in a teaching situation) must realize the mise en scène imposed by the use of speech under the simple effect of a natural determination (stemming from the physical nature of articulatory breathing). This mise en scène develops as follows. Either the speaker chooses in all good faith a role of Authority, in which case it suffices to 'speak well', in compliance with the Law present in every act of speech – without hesitation, at the right speed, clearly (which is what is demanded of good pedagogic speech: clarity, authority); the precise phrase is truly a sentence, a *sententia*, an act of penal speech. Or the speaker is bothered by all this Law that the act of speaking is going to introduce into what he wants to say, in which case, since it is impossible to alter the delivery (condemning one to 'clarity') but possible to *excuse oneself* for speaking (for laying out the Law), he uses the irreversibility of speech in order to disturb its legality: correcting, adding, wavering, the speaker moves into the infinitude of language, superimposes on the simple message that everyone expects of him a new message that ruins the very idea of a message and, through the shifting reflection of the blemishes and excesses with which he accompanies the line of the discourse, asks us to believe with him that language is not to be reduced to communication. By all these operations, which come near the wavering movement of the Text, the imperfect orator hopes to render less disagreeable the role that makes every speaker a kind of policeman. Yet at the end of all this effort to 'speak badly' another role is enforced, for the audience (nothing to do with the reader), caught in its own imaginary, receives these fumblings as so many signs of weakness and sends the speaker back the image of a master who is human, too human – *liberal*.

The choice is gloomy: conscientious functionary or free artist, the teacher escapes neither the theatre of speech nor the Law played out on its stage: the Law appears *not in what is said but in the very fact of speech.* In order to subvert the Law (and not simply get around it), the teacher would have to undermine voice delivery, word speed, and rhythm to the point of *another* intelligibility. Or not speak at all; which, however, would be to rejoin other roles again – that of the great silent mind, mute with the weight of experience, or that of the militant who in the name of praxis dismisses all discourse as futile. Nothing to be done: language is always a matter of force, to speak is to exercise a will for power; in the realm of speech there is no innocence, no safety.

The summary

Statutorily the discourse of the teacher is marked by the following characteristic: one can (one may) summarize it (a privilege it holds in common with the discourse of Members of Parliament). There is an exercise in our schools called *text reduction*,[1] a term which expresses nicely the ideology of the summary: on the one side the 'thought', object of the message, element of knowledge, transitive or critical force; on the other the 'style', ornament, province of luxury and leisure and thus futility. To separate the thought from the style is in some sort to relieve the discourse of its sacerdotal robes, to secularize the message (hence the bourgeois conjuncture of the teacher and the Member of Parliament). 'Form' is believed to be compressible and such compression is not judged essentially harmful – from a distance indeed, from our Western promontory, is the difference really so very great between the head of a living Jivaro and a shrunken Jivaro head?

It is difficult for a teacher to see the 'notes' taken during his courses. He hardly wants to, either out of discretion (nothing more personal than 'notes', despite the formal nature of the practice) or, more likely, from fear of contemplating himself in a reduced state, at once dead and substantial like a Jivaro treated by his fellows. No knowing whether what is taken (culled) from the flow of speech is scattered statements (formulae, sentences) or the gist of an argument, but in both cases what is lost is the supplement, the point of the advance of the state of language. The summary is a disavowal of writing.

In contrasting consequence, the term 'writer' (a term which here always refers to a practice, not to a social value) may be applied to any sender whose 'message' (thereby immediately destroying its very nature as message) cannot

1. [*'réduction de texte'*, i.e. a form of précis]

be summarized, a condition the writer shares with the mad-man, the chatterbox and the mathematician but which precisely writing (namely a certain practice of the signifier) has as its task to specify.

The teaching relationship

How can the teacher be assimilated to the psychoanalyst? It is exactly the contrary which is the case: the teacher is the person analysed.

Imagine that I am a teacher: I speak, endlessly, in front of and for someone who remains silent. I am the person who says *I* (the detours of *one*, *we* or impersonal sentence make no difference), I am the person who, under cover of *setting out* a body of knowledge, *puts out* a discourse, *never knowing how that discourse is being received* and thus for ever forbidden the reassurance of a definitive image – even if offensive – which would *constitute me*. In the *exposé*, more aptly named than we tend to think, it is not knowledge which is exposed, it is the subject (who exposes himself to all sorts of painful adventures). The mirror is empty, reflecting back to me no more than the falling away of my language as it gradually unrolls. Like the Marx Brothers disguised as Russian airmen (in *A Night at the Opera* – a work which I regard as allegorical of many a textual problem), I am, at the beginning of my exposé, rigged out with a large false beard which, drenched little by little with the flood of my own words (a substitute for the jug of water from which the *Mute*, Harpo, guzzles away on the Mayor of New York's rostrum), I then feel coming unstuck piecemeal in front of everybody. Scarcely have I made the audience smile with some 'witty' remark, scarcely have I reassured it with some progressive stereotype, than I experience all the complacency of such provocations; I regret the hysterical drive, would like to retract it, preferring too late an austere to a 'clever' discourse (but in that contrary case it is the 'severity' of the discourse that would seem hysterical to me). Should some smile answer my remark or some gesture of assent my stereotype of intimidation, I immediately persuade myself that these manifestations of complicity come from imbeciles or flatterers (I am here describing an imaginary process). It is I who am after a response and who let myself go as far as to provoke it, yet it suffices that I receive a response for me to become distrustful. If I develop a discourse such that it coldly averts any response, I do not thereby feel myself to be any more in *true* (in the musical sense), for I must then glory in the solitude of my speech, furnish it with the alibi of missionary discourses (science, truth, etc.).

Thus, in accordance with psychoanalytic description (Lacan's, the perspicacity of which in this respect any speaker can confirm), when the teacher speaks to his audience, the Other is always there, *puncturing* his discourse. Were the discourse held tightly fastened by an impeccable intelligence, armed with scientific 'rigour' or political radicality, it would nevertheless be punctured: it suffices that I speak, that my speech flow, for it to flow away. Naturally however, though every teacher occupies the position of a person in analysis, no student audience can claim the advantage of the opposite situation: firstly, because the psychoanalytic silence has nothing pre-eminent about it; secondly, because it happens that a subject, carried away, emerges and rushes to burn on speech, to join in the oratorical promiscuity (and should the subject remain obstinately silent, this is simply to give voice to the obstinacy of his muteness). Yet for the teacher, the student audience is still the exemplary Other in that it *has an air* of not speaking – and thus, from the bosom of its apparent flatness, speaks in you so much the louder: its implicit speech, which is mine, touches me all the more in that I am not encumbered by its discourse.

Such is the cross borne in every public act of speech. Whether the teacher speaks or whether the listener urges the right to speak, in both cases we go straight to the analytic couch: the teaching relationship is nothing more than the transference it institutes; 'science', 'method', 'knowledge', 'idea' come indirectly, are given *in addition* – they are *left-overs*.

The contract

'Most of the time, the relations between humans suffer, often to the point of destruction, from the fact that the contract established in those relations is not respected. As soon as two human beings enter into reciprocal relationship, their contract, generally tacit, comes into force, regulating the form of their relations, etc.' – Brecht

Although the demand expressed in the community space of a course is fundamentally intransitive, as is natural in any transferential situation, it is nonetheless overdetermined and shelters behind other, seemingly transitive, demands. These latter constitute the conditions of an implicit contract between the teacher and the taught, a contract which is 'imaginary', no way in contradiction with the economic determination which impels the student to be in search of a career and the teacher to fulfil the terms of an employment.

Here pell-mell (in the order of the imaginary there is no founding motive) is what the teacher demands of those taught: 1) to acknowledge him in whatever 'role' it may be – authority, benevolence, militancy, knowledge, etc. (any newcomer who cannot be placed as to the *image* he asks of you is immediately disturbing); 2) to act as relay, to extend him, to spread his style and ideas far afield; 3) to let himself be seduced, to assent to a loving relationship (granting all the sublimations, the distances, the checks consonant with the social reality and the presentiment of the futility of the relationship); 4) to allow him to honour the contract he has himself entered into with his employer, with society: the person taught is the necessary part of a (remunerated) practice, the object of a job, the matter of a production (even if difficult to define).

From his side, here pell-mell is what the person taught demands of the teacher: 1) to help him to a good professional training; 2) to fulfil the roles traditionally devolving to the teacher (scientific authority, transmission of a capital of knowledge, etc.); 3) to reveal the secrets of a technique (of research, for passing an examination); 4) under the banner of the secular saint Method, to be an instructor in ascesis, a *guru*; 5) to represent a 'movement of ideas', a School, a Cause, to be its spokesman; 6) to admit him, the student, into the complicity of a special language; 7) for those possessed by the fantasy of the thesis (a timid practice of writing, at once disfigured and shielded by its institutional finality), to guarantee the reality of that fantasy; 8) to lend service – the teacher signs registration forms, testimonials, and so on.

This is simply a topic, a fund of choices which are not necessarily all actualized at the same time in a particular individual. It is at the level of the contractual totality, however, that is decided the *comfort* of the teaching relationship: the 'good' teacher, the 'good' student are those who accept philosophically the plurality of their determinations, perhaps because they know that the truth of a relationship of speech is *elsewhere*.

Research

What is a piece of 'research'? To find out, we would need to have some idea of what a 'result' is. What is it that one finds? What is it that one wants to find? *What is missing?*

In what axiomatic field will the fact isolated, the meaning brought out, the statistical discovery be placed? No doubt it depends each time on the particular science approached, but from the moment a piece of research concerns the text (and the text extends very much further than the literary work) the research itself becomes text, production: to it, any 'result' is literally *im-pertinent*. 'Research' is then the name which prudently, under the constraint of certain social conditions, we give to the activity of writing: research here moves on the side of writing, is an adventure of the signifier, an excess of exchange – impossible to maintain the equation of a 'result' *for* a 'piece of research'. Which is why the discourse to which a piece of research must be submitted (in teaching it) has as speciality, besides its parenetic function ('*Write!*'), to recall the research to its epistemological condition: whatever it searches for, it must not forget its nature as language – and it is this which renders finally inevitable an encounter with writing. In writing, the enunciation deludes the enounced by the effect of the language which produces it, a good enough definition of the productive, dissatisfied, progressive, critical element which is indeed ordinarily granted to 'research'. Such is the historical role of research: teach the scientist or scholar *that he speaks* (but if he knew it, he would *write* – and the whole idea of science, the whole of scientificity would be changed thereby).

The destruction of stereotypes

Someone writes to me that 'a group of revolutionary students is preparing a destruction of the structuralist myth'. I am captivated by the stereotypic consistency of the expression. The destruction of the myth begins from the very announcement of its putative agents with the finest of myths, the 'group of revolutionary students' – quite as good as 'war widows' or 'old soldiers'.

Usually the stereotype is a sad affair, since it is constituted by a necrosis of language, a prosthesis brought in to fill a hole in writing. Yet at the same time it cannot but occasion a huge burst of laughter: it takes itself seriously, believes itself to be closer to the truth because indifferent to its nature as language. It is at once corny and solemn.

Setting the stereotype at a distance is not a political task, for political language is itself made up of stereotypes, but a critical task, one, that is, which aims to call language into crisis. Such an activity allows one first and foremost to isolate the speck of ideology contained in every political discourse and to attack it like an acid capable of dissolving the greasiness of 'natural' language (that is to say of language which feigns ignorance of the fact of its nature as language). It is a way too of breaking with the mechanistic conception of language as mere response to stimuli of situation or action, a way of opposing the production of language to its simple and fallacious utilization. Then again, it jolts the discourse of the Other and constitutes a permanent operation of pre-analysis. Lastly, the stereotype is at bottom a form of opportunism: one conforms to the reigning language, or rather to that in language which seems to *govern* (a situation, a right, a struggle, an institution, a movement, a science, a theory, etc.); to speak in stereotypes is to side with the power of language, an opportunism which must (today) be refused.

But is it not possible to 'transcend' stereotypes instead of 'destroying' them? The wish is unrealistic; operators of language have no other activity at their command than that of emptying what is full: language is not dialectical – it allows only a movement in two stages.

The chain of discourses

It is because language is not dialectical (does not allow the third term other than as pure oratorical flourish, rhetorical assertion, pious hope) that discourse (discursivity) moves, in its historical impetus, by *clashes*. A new discourse can only emerge as the *paradox* which goes against (and often goes for) the surrounding or preceding *doxa*, can only see the day as difference, distinction, working loose *against* what sticks to it. For example, Chomskyan theory is constructed *against* Bloomfieldian behaviourism; linguistic behaviourism once liquidated by Chomsky, it is then *against* Chomskyan mentalism (or anthropologism) that a new semiotics is being developed, while Chomsky himself, in quest of allies, is forced to *jump* over his immediate predecessors and go back as far as the Port-Royal *Grammar*. But doubtless it is in one of the greatest thinkers of dialectics, Marx, that it would be the most interesting to verify the undialectical nature of language: Marx's discourse is almost entirely *paradoxical*, the doxa being now Proudhon, now someone else, and so on. This twofold movement of separation and renewal results not in a circle but, according to Vico's great and beautiful image, in a spiral and it is in this *drift* of circularity (of paradoxical form) that historical determinations are articulated. Hence it is always necessary to establish what *doxa* an author is opposing (this can sometimes be a very minority *doxa*, holding sway over a limited group). A teaching may equally be evaluated in terms of paradox, provided it is built on the following conviction: that a system calling for corrections, translations, openings, and negations is more useful than an unformulated absence of system – one may then avoid the immobility of prattle and connect to the historical chain of discourses, the progress (*progressus*) of discursivity.

Method

Some people talk avidly, demandingly of method; what they

want in work is method, which can never be too rigorous or too formal for their taste. Method becomes a Law, but since that Law is devoid of any effect outside itself (nobody can say what a 'result' is in 'human sciences') it is infinitely disappointed; posing as a pure meta-language, it partakes of the vanity of all meta-language. The invariable fact is that a piece of work which ceaselessly proclaims its determination for method is ultimately sterile: everything has been put into the method, nothing is left for writing; the researcher repeatedly asserts that his text will be methodological but the text never comes. No surer way to kill a piece of research and send it to join the great waste of abandoned projects than Method.

The danger of Method (of a fixation with Method) is to be grasped by considering the two demands to which the work of research must reply. The first is a demand for responsibility: the work must increase lucidity, manage to reveal the implications of a procedure, the alibis of a language, in short must constitute a *critique* (remember once again that to *criticize* means *to call into crisis*). Here Method is inevitable, irreplaceable, not for its 'results' but precisely – or on the contrary – because it realizes the highest degree of consciousness of a language *which is not forgetful of itself*. The second demand, however, is of a quite different order; it is that of writing, space of dispersion of desire, where Law is dismissed. *At a certain moment*, therefore, it is necessary to turn against Method, or at least to treat it without any founding privilege as one of the voices of plurality – as a *view*, a spectacle mounted in the text, the text which all in all is the only 'true' result of any research.

Questions

To question is to want to know something. Yet in many intellectual debates the questions that follow the lecturer's talk are in no way the expression of a lack but the assertion of a plenitude. Under the cover of asking questions, I attack the speaker. *To question* then takes on its police sense: *to question* is to challenge, to interpellate. The person interpellated, however, must pretend to reply to the letter of the question, not to the manner in which it is posed. So a game is set up: although each person knows exactly what the intentions of the other really are, the game demands a reply to the content and not to the manner. If I am asked in a certain tone of voice '*What's the use of linguistics?*', thereby signifying to me that it is of no use whatsoever, I must pretend to reply naively '*It helps to do this and that,*' and not, in accordance with the truth of the dialogue, 'Why are you attacking me?' What I receive is the connotation; what I have to return is the denotation. In the space of speech, science and logic, knowledge and reasoning, questions and answers, propositions and objections are the masks of the dialectical relationship. Our intellectual debates are coded every bit as much as were the Scholastic disputations; we still have the stock roles (the 'sociologistic', the 'Goldmannian', the 'Telquelian', etc.) but contrary to the *disputatio*, where such roles would have been ceremonial and have displayed the artifice of their function, our intel███████tercourse' always gives itself 'natural' airs: it claims to exchange only signifieds, not signifiers.

In the name of what?

I speak in the name of what? Of a function? A body of knowledge? An experience? What do I represent? A scientific capacity? An institution? A service? In fact, I speak only in the name of a language: I speak because I have written; writing is represented by its contrary, by speech. This distortion means that in writing *of* speech (on the subject of speech) I am condemned to the following aporia:

denounce the imaginary of speech through the irreality of writing. Thus at this moment I am not describing any 'authentic' experience, giving the picture of any 'real' teaching, opening any 'university' dossier. For writing can tell the truth on language but not the truth on the real (we are at present trying to find out what a real without language is).

The standing position

Can one imagine a more doubtful situation than that of talking for (or in front of) people who are standing up or who are visibly badly seated? What is being exchanged here? What is this discomfort the price of? What is my speech *worth*? How could the awkwardness of the hearer's position not lead to questions as to the validity of what is being heard? Is not the standing position eminently *eritical*? And is it not thus, changing the scale, that political consciousness begins, in *un-ease*? Listening returns me the vanity of my own speech, its *price*, for, whether I like it or not, I am placed in a circuit of exchange; and listening is also the position of the person to whom I address myself.

Familiarity

It sometimes happens, remnant of May '68, that a student speaks to a teacher in the familiar *tu*-form, which gives us a strong, full sign, referring to the most psychological of signifieds: the will for militancy or mateyness – *muscle*. Since a morality of the sign is here imposed, it can be challenged in its turn and a subtler semantics preferred. Signs must be handled on a neutral ground and in French that ground is the polite *vous*-form. The *tu*-form can only break loose from the code in cases where it constitutes *a simplification of grammar* (as, for example, when talking to a foreigner with poor French). In such cases it is a matter of substituting a transitive practice for a symbolic attitude: instead of seeking to signify *just who* I think the other is (and so just who I think I am), I simply try to make myself clearly understood to him. But the strategy is also itself finally devious: the *tu*-form is like all attitudes of flight; when a sign displeases me, when the meaning bothers me, I shift towards the operational, which becomes a censorship of the symbolic and thus the symbol of asymbolism. A great many political and scientific discourses are characterized by a shift of this kind (on which depends, notably, the whole of the linguistics of 'communication').

An odour of speech

As soon as one has finished speaking, there begins the dizzying turn of the image: one exalts or regrets what one has said, the way in which one said it, one *imagines oneself* (turns oneself over in image); speech is subject to remanence, it *smells*.

Writing has no smell: produced (having accomplished its process of production), it *falls*, not like a bellows deflating but like a meteorite disappearing; it will *travel* far from my body, yet without being something detached and narcissistically retained like speech; its disappearance holds no disappointment; it passes, traverses, and that's all. The time of speech exceeds the act of speech (only a jurist could have us believe that spoken words disappear, *verba volant*). Writing, however, has no past (if society obliges you to administer what you have written, you can only do it with the most profound boredom, the boredom of a false past). Which is why the discourse applied in commenting writing has a much less striking effect than that applied in commenting speech (though the stake is greater): I can *objectively* take account of the first for 'I' am no longer there; the second, even if it is in praise, I can only try to get rid of, for it does no more than retighten he impasse of my imaginary.

(How is it then that this present text preoccupies me, that once completed, corrected, let go of, the text remains or returns in me as a state of doubt and, in a word, of fear? Is it not *written*, liberated by writing? I see that I cannot improve the piece, I have achieved the exact form of what I wanted to say; it is no longer a question of *style*. I conclude, therefore, that it is the very status of the piece which disturbs me; what plagues me in it is precisely that, dealing with speech, it cannot, *in writing itself*, fully liquidate speech. In order to write *of* speech (about speech) I am compelled to *refer* to illusions of experiences, memories, and feelings had by the subject I am when I speak, that I was when speaking: in such a writing the referential lingers on and it is that which smells to my own nostrils.)

Our place

Just as psychoanalysis, with the work of Lacan, is in the process of extending the Freudian topic into a topology of the subject (the unconscious is never there in *its* place), so likewise we need to substitute for the magisterial space of the past – which was fundamentally a religious space (the word delivered by the master from the pulpit above with the audience below, the flock, the sheep, the herd) – a less upright, less Euclidean space where no one, neither teacher nor students, would ever be *in his final place*. One would then be able to see that what must be made reversible are not social 'roles' (is there any point in squabbling for 'authority', for the 'right' to speak?) but the regions of speech. Where is speech? In locution? In listening? In the *returns* of the one and the other? The problem is not to abolish the distinction in functions (*teacher/student* – after all, as Sade has taught us, order is one of the guarantees of pleasure) but to protect the instability and, as it were, the giddying whirl of the positions of speech. In the teaching space nobody should anywhere be in his place (I am comforted by this constant displacement: were I to *find my place*, I would not even go on pretending to teach, I would give up).

Yet is it not the case that the teacher has a fixed place, that of his *remuneration*, the place he occupies in the economy, in production? We come back to the same problem, our sole and continuing concern: the origin of a spoken discourse does not exhaust that discourse; once set off, it is beset by a thousand adventures, its origin becomes blurred, all its effects are not in its cause. It is this *excess* which here concerns us.

Two types of criticism

The mistakes that may be made in typing out a manuscript are so many meaningful incidents, incidents which by analogy help to shed light on the attitude it is necessary to adopt with regard to meaning when commenting a text.

Either the word produced by the mistake (if spoilt by a wrong letter) has no meaning, finds no textual contour, in which case the code is interrupted, creating an asemic word, a pure signifier; for example, instead of writing *officier* [officer] I write *offivier* which is meaningless. Or the erroneous – mistyped – word, though not the word one intended to write, is a word identifiable in the lexicon, a word which means something: should I write *ride* [wrinkle] instead of *rude* [rude, rough], the new word exists in French and the sentence retains a meaning, even if eccentric. This is the choice (the voice?) of pun, anagram, semantic metathesis, spoonerism: there is a sliding *within the codes* – meaning remains but pluralized, cheated, without law of content, message, truth.

Each of these two types of mistake figures (or prefigures) a type of criticism. The first dismisses all meaning of the support text which is to lend itself only to a signifying efflorescence: its phonism alone is to be treated, but not interpreted; one associates, one does not decipher. Giving the reading *offivier* as opposed to *officier*, the mistake opens up for me the *right of association* – I am free to explode *offivier* towards *obvier* [obviate], *vivier* [fish stock], etc. It is not simply that the ear of this first criticism hears the cracklings of the phono pick-up but rather that it desires to hear only them, making them into a new music. In the second type of criticism nothing is rejected by the 'reading head'; it perceives both the meaning (the meanings) and its cracklings. The (historical) stake of these two types of criticism (I should like to be able to say that the field of the first is *signifiosis* and that of the second *signifiance*) is clearly different.

The first has in its favour the right of the signifier to spread out where it will (where it can?): what law, and what meaning, and with what basis, would restrain it? Once the philological (monological) law has been relaxed and the text eased open to plurality, why stop? Why refuse to push polysemy as far as asemy? In the name of what? Like any radical right, this one supposes a utopian vision of freedom: the law is lifted *all at once*, outside of any history, in defiance of any dialectic (hence the finally petit-bourgeois aspect of this style of demand). Yet the moment it evades all tactical reason while nevertheless remaining implanted in a specific (and alienated) intellectual society, the disorder of the signifier reverts into hysterical rambling: liberating reading from all meaning, it is ultimately *my* reading which I impose, for in *this* moment of History the economy of the subject is not yet transformed and the refusal of meaning (of meanings) falls back into subjectivity. At best, one can simply say that this radical criticism, defined by a fore-closure of the signified (and not by its slide), *anticipates* History, anticipates a new, unprecedented state in which the efflorescence of the signifier would not be at the cost of any idealist counterpart, of any closure of the person. To criticize, however, is to put into crisis, something which is not possible without evaluating the conditions of the crisis (its limits), without considering its historical moment. Thus the second type of criticism, that which applies itself to the division of meanings and the 'trickery' of interpretation, appears (at least to me) more historically correct. In a society locked in the war of meanings and thereby under the compulsion of rules of communication which determine its effectiveness, the liquidation of the old criticism can only be carried forward *in* meaning (in the volume of meanings) and not outside it. In other words, it is necessary to practice a certain semantic enterism. Ideological criticism is today precisely condemned to operations of theft: the signified, exemption of which is the materialist task par excellence, is more easily 'lifted' in the *illusion* of meaning than in its destruction.

Two types of discourse

Let us distinguish two types of discourse:

Terrorist discourse is not necessarily bound up with the peremptory assertion (or the opportunist defence) of a faith, a truth, a certain justice; it can simply be the wish to accomplish the lucid adequation of the enunciation with the true violence of language, the inherent violence which stems from the fact that no utterance is able directly to express the truth and has no other mode at its disposal than the force of the word; thus an apparently terrorist discourse ceases to be so if, reading it, one follows the directions it itself provides, re-establishing in it the gap or dispersion, that is to say the unconscious. Such a reading is not always easy: certain small-scale terrorisms which function above all by stereotypes themselves operate, like any discourse of good conscience, the foreclosure of the other scene; in short, these terrorisms *refuse writing* (they can be detected by something in them that remains rigid – the odour of seriousness given off by the commonplace).

Repressive discourse is not linked to declared violence but to the Law. The Law here enters language as equilibrium: an equilibrium is postulated between what is forbidden and what is permitted, between commendable meaning and unworthy meaning, between the constraint of common sense and the probationary freedom of interpretations. Hence the taste shown by such discourse for motions of balance, verbal opposites, antitheses formulated and evaded, being *neither* for this *nor* for that (if, however, you do the double addition of the *neithers* and *nors*, it will be seen that our *impartial*, *objective*, *human* speaker is *for* this, against *that*). Repressive discourse is the discourse of good conscience, liberal discourse.

The axiomatic field

'All that is necessary', comments Brecht, 'is to determine those interpretations of facts appearing within the proletariat engaged in the class struggle (national or international) which enable it to utilize the facts for its action. They must be synthesized in order to create an axiomatic field.' Thus every fact possesses several meanings (a plurality of 'interpretations') and amongst those meanings there is one which is proletarian (or at least which is of use to the proletariat in its struggle); by connecting the various proletarian meanings one constructs a revolutionary axiomatics. But who determines the meaning? According to Brecht, the proletariat itself (*'appearing within the proletariat'*). Such a view implies that class division has its inevitable counterpart in a division of meanings and class struggle its equally inevitable counterpart in a war of meanings: so long as there is class struggle (national or international), the division of the axiomatic field will be inexpiable.

The difficulty (despite Brecht's verbal assurance – *'All that is necessary'*) comes from the fact that a certain number of objects of discourse do not directly concern the proletariat (they find no interpretation within it) which cannot, however, remain indifferent to them, since they constitute, at least in advanced States which have wiped out both misery and folklore, the plenitude of the other discourse within which the very proletariat is compelled to live, nourish, and amuse itself. This discourse is that of culture (it is possible that in Marx's day the pressure of culture on the proletariat was weaker than it is now; in the absence of 'mass communications', there was as yet no 'mass culture'). How can you attribute a meaning for the struggle to something of no direct concern to you? How could the proletariat determine *within itself* an interpretation of Zola, Poussin, pop music, the Sunday sports paper or the latest news item? To 'interpret' all these cultural relays it needs *representatives* – those whom Brecht calls the 'artists' or the 'workers of the intellect' (a particularly malicious expression, at least in French where the intellect is so nearly off the top of the head), those who have at their command the language of the indirect, the indirect as language; in a word, *oblates* who devote themselves to the proletarian interpretation of cultural facts.

Then begins, however, for these procurators of proletarian meaning, a real headache of a problem since their class situation is not that of the proletariat: they are not producers, a negative situation they share with (student) youth – an equally unproductive class with whom they usually form an alliance of language. It follows that the culture from which they have to disengage the proletarian meaning brings them back round to themselves and not to the proletariat. How is culture to be *evaluated*? According to its origin? Bourgeois. Its finality? Bourgeois again. According to dialectics? Although bourgeois, this does contain progressive elements; but what, *at the level of discourse*, distinguishes dialectics from compromise? And then again, with what instruments? Historicism, sociologism, positivism, formalism, psychoanalysis? Every one of them bourgeoisified. There are some who finally prefer to give up the problem, to dismiss all 'culture' – a course which entails the destruction of all discourse.

In fact, even within an axiomatic field thought to be clarified by the class struggle, the tasks are various, occasionally contradictory, and, most importantly, established on different temporalities. The axiomatic field is made up of several specific axiomatics: cultural criticism proceeds *successively, diversely and simultaneously* by opposing the Old with the New, historicism with sociologism, formalism with economism, psychoanalysis with logico-positivism, and then again, *by a further turn*, empirical sociology with monumental history, the New with the strange (the foreign), historicism with formalism, scientism with psychoanalysis, and so on. Applied to culture, critical discourse can only be a silk shot through with tactics, a tissue of elements now past, now circumstantial (linked to contingencies of fashion), now finally and frankly utopian. To the tactical necessities of the war of meanings is added the strategic conception of the new conditions which will be given the signifier when that war comes to an end. Cultural criticism, that is, must be *impatient*, it cannot be carried on without desire. Hence all the discourses of Marxism are present in its writing: the apologetic (glorify revolutionary science), the apocalyptic (destroy bourgeois culture), and the eschatological (desire and call for the undivision of meaning, concomitant on class undivision).

Our unconscious

The problem posed is this: how can the two great *epistemes* of modernity, namely the materialist and the Freudian dialectics, be made to intersect, to unite in the production of a new human relation (it is not to be excluded that a third term may be hidden in the inter-diction of the first two)? That is to say: how can we aid the inter-action of these two desires – to change the economy of the relations of production and to change the economy of the subject? (For the moment psychoanalysis appears to be the force best fitted for the second of the tasks but other topics can be imagined, those of the East for example.)

The path of this comprehensive work lies through the following question: what is the relation between class determination and the unconscious? By what displacement does this determination slip in between subjects? Certainly not by 'psychology' (as though there were mental contents – bourgeois/proletarian/intellectual/etc.) but quite obviously by language, by discourse: the Other – who speaks, who is all speech – is social. On the one hand, the proletariat may well be *separated* but it is still bourgeois language, in its degraded petit-bourgeois form, which speaks unconsciously in the proletariat's cultural discourse; on the other, the proletariat may well be mute but it still speaks in the discourse of the intellectual, not as canonical founding voice but as unconscious. It suffices in this respect to see how it *knocks* on all our discourses (explicit reference by the intellectual to the proletariat in no way prevents the latter from occupying the place of the unconscious in our discourse). Only the bourgeois discourse of the bourgeoisie is tautological: the unconscious of bourgeois discourse is indeed the Other, but that Other in another bourgeois discourse.

Writing as value

Evaluation precedes criticism. There is no putting into crisis without evaluation. Our value is writing, an obstinate reference which, apart from the fact that it must often irritate, seems in the eyes of some to involve a risk – that of developing a certain *mystique*. The reproach has its malice, for it reverses point by point the importance we attach to writing, regarded, in this tiny intellectual region of our Western world, as *the materialist field par excellence*. Though issuing from Marxism and psychoanalysis, the theory of writing tries to displace – without breaking with – that place of origin: on the one hand, it rejects the temptation of the signified, that is the deafness to language, to the excessive return of its effects; on the other, it is opposed to speech in that it is not transferential and outplays – admittedly partially, in extremely narrow, particularist social limits even – the traps of 'dialogue'. There is in writing the beginnings of a mass gesture: against all discourses (modes of speech, instrumental writings, rituals, protocols, social symbolics), writing alone today, even if still in the form of luxury, makes of language something *atopical*, without place. It is this dispersion, this unsituation, which is materialist.

Peaceable speech

One of the things that can be expected from a regular meeting together of speakers is quite simply *goodwill*, that the meeting figure a space of discourse divested of all sense of aggressiveness.

Such a divestiture arouses resistances. The first is of a

cultural nature: the refusal of violence is commonly seen as a humanist lie, courtesy (minor mode of that refusal) as a class value and openness as a mystification related to the liberal idea of dialogue. The second resistance is of an imaginary order: many people want a conflictual discourse from motives of psychic liberation; the removal of confrontation is said to have something frustrating about it. The third resistance is of a political order: polemic is an essential arm in the struggle, any space of discourse must be splintered in order that its contradictions may emerge – it must be kept under scrutiny.

What is preserved in these three resistances, however, is ultimately the unity of the neurotic subject, which *comes together* in the forms of conflict. Yet we know that violence is always there (in language) and it is precisely this that can lead us to decide to bracket out its signs and thus to dispense with a rhetoric; violence must not be absorbed by the code of violence.

The first advantage of this would be to suspend or at least to delay the roles of speech – so that listening, speaking, replying, I never be the actor of a judgement, a subjection, an intimidation, the advocate of a Cause. No doubt peaceable speech will finally secrete its own role, since, whatever I say, the other continues to read me as an image; but in the time put into eluding such a role, in the work of language accomplished by the community week after week towards the abolition from its discourse of all stichomythia, a certain dispropriation of speech (from then on close to writing) may be attained – or again, *a certain generalization of the subject*.

Perhaps this is what is found in certain experiences with drugs (in the experience of certain drugs). Though not smoking oneself (if only because of bronchial inability to inhale the smoke), it is impossible to remain insensible to the general goodwill that pervades certain places abroad where cannabis is smoked. The movements, the (few) words spoken, the whole relationship of the bodies (a relationship nevertheless immobile and distant), everything is relaxed, disarmed (hence totally unlike drunkenness, the legal form of violence in the West); the space seems to be the product of a subtle ascesis (one can sometimes read in it a certain *irony*). A meeting for speech should, I think, aim at this *suspension* (no matter of what – the desire is for a form), try to rejoin an *art of living*, the greatest of all the arts according to Brecht (such a view is more dialectical than it appears, in that it compels the distinction and evaluation of the customs of violence). In short, within the very limits of the teaching space as given, the need is to work at patiently tracing out a pure form, that of a *floating* (the very form of the signifier); a floating which would not destroy anything but would be content simply to disorientate the Law. The necessities of promotion, professional obligations (which nothing then prevents from being scrupulously fulfilled), imperatives of knowledge, prestige of method, ideological criticism – everything is there, but *floating*.

Index

Far from any idea of 'exhaustiveness' or the imposition of an 'order', this index aims merely to provide a few points of reference for some of the terms and concepts that occur in the essays collected here. Evidently, notions such as Writing, Subject, Text are developed constantly throughout the collection and can receive only token entries; proper names have been included solely when they stand for a textual practice important for that development.

Course in General Linguistics

Ferdinand de Saussure

Ferdinand de Saussure died in 1913 with his masterpiece, *Cours de linguistique générale* still unwritten. Only in 1916 was a text reconstructed and published from his students' notes. But since then Saussure has been recognized as not only the founder of modern linguistics, but a formative influence on the development of twentieth-century thought.

In *Course in General Linguistics* Saussure defines those distinctions that have provided the basis for all subsequent linguistic studies. The book is a classic of intellectual discovery, whose more general implications are only now being widely recognized. As Jonathan Culler writes in his introduction: 'Saussure helps us to understand the role played by distinctions which structure our world and the systems of convention by which man becomes *homo significans*, a creature who gives things meaning.'

Keywords

Raymond Williams

Alienation, creative, family, media, radical, structural, taste: these
are seven of the hundred or so words whose derivation, development and contemporary meaning Raymond Williams explores
in this unique study of the language in which we discuss 'culture'
and 'Society'.

A series of connecting essays investigate how these 'key-
words' have been formed, redefined, confused and reinforced as
the historical contexts in which they were applied changed to
give us their current meaning and significance.

'This is a book which everyone who is still capable of being
educated should read.'   Christopher Hill, *New Society*

'. . . for the first time we have some of the materials for constructing a genuinely historical and a genuinely social semantics
. . . Williams's book is unique in its kind so far and it provides a
model as well as a resource for us all.'

Alasdair MacIntyre, *New Statesman*

Illuminations

Walter Benjamin

'From the evidence of this book I would suggest that Benjamin was one of the great European writers of this century.'
Philip Toynbee, *Observer*

Only since his death have Benjamin's works – literary essays, general reflections, aphorisms and probings into cultural phenomena – achieved fame outside his native Germany, where a discerning audience had already recognised him as one of the most acute and original minds of his time.

This aptly named collection includes Benjamin's views on Kafka, Baudelaire and Proust, essays on Leskov and Brecht's Epic Theatre, and discussions on art, technology and mass society, translation as a literary mode, and the philiosophy of history.

In her introduction Hannah Arendt presents the critic's personality and intellectual development as well as placing his life and work in the context of Hitler's Germany.